LIVING

A SIX MONTH ODYSSEY

ALLEGRETA BLAU

outskirts press

PARIS!

May 5, 2001 — Saturday, 9:30

Dreaming, fantasizing, idle conversation – thus began Our Epic Journey a year ago. But where exactly to begin? Paris, mais oui. Exciting and exhausting just like New York City, my home town. The weather is awful. It is cold, dark and windy. Just like New York City in the Winter. My home town. And it's Spring. Why are we here? What got us here?

The idea for this grand adventure started out very innocently. My husband Peter and I were in Paris a few years ago and thought we would one day soon like to spend at least six months in Europe. We were well into middle age and time was a'wastin.' And so about six months ago, we sold our house, packed up all our belongings to put in storage, had an estate sale of our furniture, and then packed for Europe. We were ready. We made reservations for hotel stays in

I

Paris, London and Rome, the cities we knew we definitely wanted to visit, got plane tickets and off we went. Saying goodbye to the house I lived in for twenty years was sad but knowing there would be adventures ahead, I let the sadness pass.

After a long plane ride, we arrived in Paris about 4 pm on Friday. Before we left, at the airport in Los Angeles we had to divide our clothes from our suitcases. We didn't really know how to pack for a six-month trip so we overdid it. Our cases were too heavy and we were not going to be allowed to get on the plane with the very large duffel bag. The airline people provided us with a large cardboard box. I am in the middle of International terminal at LAX among thousands of people, going through suitcases and putting stuff into one big box. The plane ride was thankfully uneventful.

We arrived finally, in Paris! We opened the box and put the clothes back into the very heavy suitcases. After a long cab ride, we arrived at Citadines, our home for the next three months. Citadines Republique is one of several Citadines in Paris. Citadines are hotel/apartments, each room has a kitchen. As it turned out, Republique was the best area for us to be in, accessible by close metro to every part of Paris and environs.

Happily, the rooms are larger than we expected. I found out later that we have the largest unit. They probably gave us this because we committed to a three month stay. We have two nice size rooms with enough closet space for us (just!) I can't see how this would work for four people, although there is sleeping for four. The rooms are plain, clean and quiet. I bought some tulips today to enhance the ambiance. We have the tiniest kitchen with every appliance save a dishwasher but no space to store or cook food. The French buy fresh food daily so do not require anything but the smallest refrigerator or cupboards. We have many dishes and cups. The living room contains Formica type furniture and a trundle bed. Think Ikea. I will take pictures.

At first, I hated it (very Motel 6 like) but it is very livable and we can go into separate rooms if necessary. This proved to be ultimately important as we are together 24/7. The bed is very comfortable. We have large windows. The walls are bare but I plan on buying prints and plants. We went right out to dinner at a brasserie two doors away. It is small and very unpretentious. Nice enough. We had spaghetti and salad. The TV was on to a French cartoon show. The owner's young son was watching it and it was very loud. We got up to leave and he turned it down. I went to the bathroom and Peter said while I was gone the owner turned it up again.

Two couples and a young girl sat down next to us. They knew the owner very well — it turns out that one of the men is a dentist in the area. I started talking to them asking them "Parlez-vous Anglais?" and the woman said yes and we started chatting. So now I am talking French as well as English! They were very warm and friendly and we told them our story. "We are going to Deauville for a long weekend as Tuesday is a national holiday in France" one of the ladies said. The French take long weekend holidays a lot. They know how to live and they don't work very hard, or so we were told.

The dentist's first name was Elie. "Wow. Same as my father's" I told him. I found out later that they were Jews and Moroccans way back. We went back to our apartment and got to bed dead tired at 10:30 pm. We are in a working class neighborhood where, we discovered quickly, very few people speak English. This venue is a combination hotel/apartment arrangement. There is a front desk with a concierge, a very small lobby, a laundry room and at sublevel there is an adorable little café, open just for breakfast. And in the lower hallway, a phone booth. We are just a few feet away from le metro and lots of markets and restaurants and bars.

We awoke at 4:00 a.m. and could no longer sleep due to jet lag, so we got out of bed and unpacked. We fell back to sleep at 8:30 in the morning. Xavier called us at 11:00 a.m. He picked us up at 12:30 and we walked around the neighborhood and then ate at a brasserie. Peter and I know already that we are going to have a difficult time with food here. It was our first meal of the day and we had to choose from lunch food. Peter had a tuna salad and I picked at pommes frites and a hardboiled egg.

A few words about Xavier. He is literally our savior. A man in his 20's, we met him on our first trip to Paris on the metro. He was helpful and friendly and after getting some logistics straight, we exchanged phone numbers and made plans to get together in Paris. After that time, we became like family, Xavier visiting us in the States and every trip after to Paris (there was three before this big one) we saw Xavier. And now, in planning the big trip, he was right there for us. Such a sweetie.

We ended up after a few excursions going to a mall in a suburb. Xavier drove us in his funny little French car, teeny tiny but not a Smart car. We went into what had to be one of the largest markets in the world, a la Costco times 10. It sold EVERYTHING — clothes, furniture and in the center, there was a huge food market. Huge! Aisles and aisles of every kind of food imaginable. I hated it. Crowded and noisy and smelled of sweat. "Keep your purse close to you," Xavier told me, "Unless you are prepared to speak French." I got the message. We went back to the apartment. Dinner was brioche and tea. We are both tres fatigue as we still have jet lag. Impressions of Paris demain. Bonne Nuit.

May 5, 2001 — Sunday, 9:30 PM

We had a bad night. Went to bed at 10:30 and slept until 2:00 a.m. We both are awake and could not go back to sleep. I took a sleeping pill. Peter got up and read. I was very nervous. My mind was going a mile a minute. I was questioning everything. Was this a good move or not? All kinds of demons. I was very anxious. Mind racing. Awful. Peter came back to bed about 5:00 a.m. and we both fell asleep. I was going crazy. Twelve hours in bed. Merde!

Boulevard Richard Lenoir is a very wide street near us. Every Tuesday and Saturday it holds a nice size open air market. The Boulevard borders a park and is quite lovely. We left for the Richard

Lenoir market at 11:30. Could not find the food we wanted, except for fabulous fruit, but there was a lot of flea market kind of stuff and resplendent with flower bouquets. Nothing I wanted to buy. Yet. Went to the local supermarche, just a few doors down from our apartment. Got some more fruits and fish. Returned to the apartment in a daze. Went out again on a metro to the Marais. I felt better seeing all the people and the art on the street and music everywhere.

The Marais is a very hip artsy area in Paris. At one time populated mostly by Jews; there is a very large old synagogue there. Now the area is full of smart shops and the Picasso Museum is in walking distance. We went into a deli called Finkelstein. I had coffee and strudel. Sitting down was heavenly. We walked some more and came upon street musicians, all playing violins and cellos, eight in all. Very wonderful stuff.

Back on to another metro to the Champs Elysees. We walk, we metro, we walk, we metro. Sometimes we bus. It was quite thrilling to see the Arc de Triomphe again. Visited the Mayflower Hotel which is one street behind the Champs Elysees, where we stayed last year and encountered Werner, the desk clerk we remembered. "Hi Werner! Comme ca va?" He remembered us too and we chatted a while. We will meet him for coffee on a Friday, which is his day off.

People are great. The Parisians get a bum rap. We are talking to everyone and mostly in French. I spoke three languages today, Spanish, French and English. There is much excitement in Paris.

It smells different here. Food is frustrating for us. We need to find our special restaurant. Have mixed emotions. I need sleep desperately. I need to feel at home and this will take some time. Tomorrow we go shopping for things for the apartment. I feel very cut off without email. Peter is a good pal. Bonne Nuit, which means good night if you haven't guessed by now.

May 7, 2001 — Monday, 11:30 PM

Okay. It's day four. This is definitely going to be a grand adventure. We still have horrible jet lag. We go to sleep around 10:30 p.m. and then wake up at 2:00 a.m. exhausted but wide awake. Last night we made it to 4:00 a.m. Peter gets up and reads in the other room and I just lay like a lox waiting for blissful sleep and my mind going, going, and going. So much STUFF has occurred for us in this short time. Being a "habitant" is a lot more difficult than being a tourist. As a tourist, the biggest decisions you have to make are where to have dinner, what museum to visit, what site to see and where to shop for things you absolutely don't need.

As people who are attempting to live here, we have many frustrations, which lead to much exhaustion. Namely, where to buy the things, you actually need. In an attempt to make this comfortable but impersonal apartment more livable, I made a list of few things I'd like to get to spice up the joint — a tablecloth, some posters, a few vases, flowers, a plant or two.

Easy stuff, right? The nearest Kmart or Target would handle these needs in a few minutes time. Not at all easy here. I checked out some stores listed in Fodor's tour books and to my chagrin they either didn't carry what was advertised, or they were beyond expensive. This, after making errors with regard to which metro to take, and walking, walking, walking, all over the place. I love the metro, and once you get on the correct one, life is a breeze.

However! If you get on the wrong one, it not only means getting off it also means walking MILES underground through various walkways and tunnels to get to the right metro train. This is because only one train (one#) rides on one rail. Not like NY where several different trains stop at the same station.

And every train seems to be in the bowels of the earth, which requires stairs, stairs, stairs — up and down up and down. There is an actual escalator at our metro stop. Yes! Our street is Parmentier. In time we found that it is broken at least 50% of the time which means a lot of stairs to walk up, at the end of the day when I am the most tired. Also, speaking a barely understandable French, a lot is misunderstood and directions we get are wrong. It is true that a lot of people speak English, but not all. When I speak French to someone, if they speak any English at all, they answer me in English. This tells me that they understand my French but my ego is still crushed! I would like to speak French tout le temps but it is not meant to be. I am getting better at it— the more I hear the more I seem to pick up. I think my New York accent throws them off. The Parisians decidedly do not think outside the box.

For example — finding certain foods. Finding flea markets. Where do you buy thumbtacks? How do I find a yoga class? Where does Peter find a place to play basketball? The concierge is of no help. If we were strictly tourists, and here for a short time, none of the above would be of consequence. But we want to do what we like wherever we are. As much as possible, that is. Spoiled Americans.

Tonight, Xavier and Corinne, his lady, came over and spent two hours setting up the internet for us. Peter is out with them now having dinner. We have maid service, once a week, demain (Mardi). I tell Peter "I am cleaning up for the maid, just like I do at home," putting stuff away, etc. This is no easy task. This place is smallish and unless everything is put away immediately it looks messy. Neither of us wants this, so we are constantly putting things away, tired as we get. I sound bitchy. But I sure do appreciate having a clean-living space.

I have not felt the glow and flow of being in Paris. We did visit the Marais yesterday — Sunday — and I loved it. Today we went to the Louvre's poster shop because we couldn't find posters anywhere else which is hard to believe.

The lower level of the Louvre is an entire city unto itself. Shops, restaurants, a cafeteria and spending, spending, spending. Actually, it's a great place but so very crowded. And the tourist season has yet to begin.

Tomorrow we take a rest from chores (can't do much in that area anyway because it is a holiday) — the day the war ended in France. We are going to L'Etoile (better known as the Arc de Triomphe) to see a parade and a ceremony where the President of the Republic will appear. That is if we can deal with the crowds. Then, to a "nice" area to see nicely dressed people (away from the metro grunge). Maybe the Left Bank. We'll see.

This city is beyond gorgeous and rich with things to do, places to go, and most of all, l'histoire.

May 8, 2001 — Tuesday night, around 10 PM — I think

It has been a heavy day for me. We walked (what else is new) back from the Republique metro station. It is s just one stop away from Parmentier, where we live. I took a very hot bath and went to bed. Peter went to bed also and lucky for him, he slept. I did not but I rested.

We went to L'Etoile this morning to see the ceremony of VE day. It was quite thrilling. We viewed the very impressive parade of all of the armed forces and the President came by in a big black limo, his arm out of the window, waving to the crowd. Of course, it could have been anyone's arm! We walked down the Champs-Elysees and I had a coffee at a kiosk in the park. We sat on a bench in the sun and it was quite pleasant, the first bit of sun we've seen since we got here. Peter fell asleep. Promptly. So, what else is new. I wanted to have a lunch at a chic place in the rue Royal, near the Palace Hotel, where Princess Diana stayed with Dodi, but Peter balked because the prices were high and I got pissed at this. I think that I will have to do this kind of stuff on my own, which is fine with me.

We took a metro to the Republique area because to stay where we were we would only encounter more expensive little wonderful cafes. Ah well... We had pizza at a local place, which at the onset I liked a lot (I was starving by then — it was 3:00 p.m.) -- but after a bit I started to feel uneasy. All that cheese. Yuck.

Shopped at Tati, a greater and smaller version of Walmart and got a few things for the apartment; two tablecloths at 10 francs each ($1.50!) a large yellow sheet to cover the couch in the living room with and a few vases. Now, where do I find thumbtacks for the prints we bought?

An observation — the Parisians must have three hands — one to hold the cell phone, one to hold the cigarette, and one to hold the leash that the dog is attached to. I don't know how they do it, but they do it. And with style.

We came back and the room hadn't been cleaned. The kitchen is a disaster to work in — making toast and tea is a major accomplishment.

I don't feel the fun has really started. We are still working on logistics. I need to know for example, how to make a phone call. No coins here, you must have a phone card. We have the Internet now but it is tres cher so we will be going to cyber cafes. I am looking forward to this experience.

I really miss television. I have to admit this! Tonight while tired, I would like to lie in bed and watch good, bad or indifferent television. Right now, we have the local HBO on and it is a movie with Dustin Hoffman and John Travolta, dubbed in in French, naturellement. I hope I sleep tonight and feel lots better tomorrow.

Bonne Nuit.

May 9, 2001 — Wednesday night, 9:45 PM

We arose late. At least I did. "Peter, it's 5:30 a.m! What are you doing?" No answer from Peter. We had breakfast here and I had a pounding headache — I feared a sinus/cold thing was going to happen. We went for a leisurely walk in the neighborhood and stopped at a café to have our very first croissants of the trip — they were fabulously delicious and I had a café au lait. Coffee tastes a whole lot better here. They care. Sorry Americans, it's true.

On to the Town Hall. Every arrondissement, or district has one — it is sort of a mini city hall where one can get all kinds of info, including marriage licenses! We got some information regarding basketball games and yoga classes but that was about it.

Had a minor disaster today. In an attempt to move some furniture, the whole thing fell on Peter and it was quite a mess. We broke the entertainment unit, which is made of pegboard but put it back together and only hope that the powers that be don't discover the mess.

I tried to make the place prettier. Bought some lilacs from a street vendor and now there is a small lace cloth, the flowers, a basket of fruit, a bottle of wine and a baguette of bread on the table, and put a poster up. Ambiance is everything. My typing is sucky because the table is too high for the computer. Tomorrow we go back to the cyber joint then we plan on taking a bus ride to the Left Bank better known as Rive Gauche, maybe, or to Bercy which is a newly developed park and monument area. Alors! A telephone call! Bonne Nuit.

May 10, 2001 — Thursday, 10 PM

This bus takes us to the Left Bank to St-Germain des Pres. We walked a lot around there and I found my Fragonard perfume and also picked up Betty's pants at a shop nearby. Does this mean I have to shlep them throughout Europe? Probably. Betty is a good friend so I won't complain. We sought the Sorbonne and after many errors, found it. We walked around the halls a little. it is an astounding place, huge in size, and I don't know what else to say about it really. We were on our way back when we happened on a cybershop. I told Peter we should try it even though we had a really bad experience at one near our apartment. It worked. He loved it. Loved it. We spent almost two hours on the internet —me, about twenty minutes and he the rest of the time. Doing business. Normal.

After we ate at a very sweet little restaurant next door where we were the only customers at 7:30 at night. The bill came to less than $20 which is great, but we are having a big problem with food here. Already. We do not eat the sauces and we don't eat meat. We had fish twice today. No one knows from scrambled eggs. And a good deli would be nice. We are decidedly not gourmets and prefer plain food, but where to find this? Vegetarian restaurants are practically nonexistent according to all the guides. And where are the health food stores? Surely in such a large city they exist.

"Let's go to the Luxembourg Gardens," I say. We took a lovely stroll and came upon a group of teenagers playing basketball. Then, all the not so much fun stuff, finding a metro. We walked and walked and walked and then once we found one it was three changes and more walking, up and down stairs. I don't like this at all. I am too tired and too old. I am going to walk, take the bus, or take taxis. Tomorrow we plan on going to L'Orangerie Musee in the am to see a Picasso exhibit, then maybe a picnic in the Tuilleries followed by a bus ride. Sounds perfect. No metros for me demain!

May 11, 2001 — Friday, 8:00 PM —

Just finished dinner. We did a bunch of non-memorable things today. The sun came out with a vengeance and it is officially HOT. Gloriously hot. We decided, after a picnic in the Tuilleries, to take a bus to anywhere. We did and there was no air-conditioning and no seats. We took a few other buses, and did a bit better and then ended up in the metro to return here and the people in the car we were in stank. So much for the loveliness of Paris.

Peter and I both feel we need to meet some people and do some things to excite us. Just roaming around is fine if you've never been here before but we need activity and structure. It is very difficult to get this here. "Let's find a yoga class for me and a place where you can play basketball." Easier said than done.

Tried to go to an American movie tonight and they are far away, requiring a metro. Also, they get the movies later here and we have seen just about everything that is showing. So, no telly, no movies and we are having difficulty with the food. I walk miles each day yet my diet is so bad — lots of bread and dairy for want of anything else. So, I am blowing up and it is distressing.

The Nanny rerun is on dubbed in French and I am watching it. That's how desperate I am. Oh well ... will work on making it all better. It's everyone's dream to live in Paris, n'est-ce pas?

May 12, 2001 — Saturday, 8:10 PM — a much better day!

What would we do without our excellent friend Xavier, I cannot imagine. He came over this a.m. and spent about two hours with us setting up the internet once more. Peter will use hotmail.com and I will still use AOL even though it costs a lot more. I don't care. I want the convenience and ease of AOL and will use it, hopefully, with discrimination. I received quite a few emails and I will attend to these in a day or two.

We had lunch "in the hood" and it was the best meal I've had thus far —a very good salad with lots of veggies and some cheese. Peter had an oceania salad with much seafood and gave me some of his shrimps. We attempted to go to an American church today and the bus turned into another direction. We changed our plans and impulsively hopped on a hop on hop off bus. This is a bus that just goes around and around the city over and over again, stopping at the big tourist attractions. You can pick it up whenever you want, wherever you want. We adored it as we went to the very top deck and sat in the very first row with all of Paris at our feet. We did not get out until the bus returned to the place where we picked it up. This trip that took two hours.

Paris is teeming with people and cars, cars, cars. I've not seen anything like it, not in Los Angeles or New York City. Thousands of these little itty-bitty cars going like bats out of hell. Today was the best weather day in Paris. The sun was shining and the temperature was in the 80's so as our friend told us, everyone came out. It has been dreadful weather since January, so the first nice Saturday sees all the natives in the parks, walking, shopping, doing, and of course eating, eating, eating. Tons of brasseries and cafes everywhere!

Okay. Or should I say alors! A little close observation here. Chic. All over the world Paris is known a as the fashion capital of the world. All the chic women and dashing looking men. Well, mon amies, it ain't so! It is chic, I am convinced, to be un-chic. In fact, the very young women, of high school and college age, are the most chic because they look the most disreputable. Our bag ladies at home would be the most chic of them all! It appears as if the clothes come out of dumpsters, some are torn, and a size smaller than they should be. And of course, only one color will do --black. Hair is barely combed. No woman wears jewelry or makeup. Xavier says these are very wealthy girls. Hard to understand. They work very hard at seeming not to care about fashion. I don't know who are buying the clothes you see in the stores (gorgeous beyond words) because they are not in evidence on the streets or in the cafes.

You can tell a tourist because she will be wearing earrings and lipstick. I did not wear either today and feel more in tune. But I refuse to wear black all the time. Too depressing.

Peter has a nose for markets. He can be lost most of the time, but he smells out food places! I think he's made a run to the local marche every day this past week. We have the tiniest of kitchens so I am hoping he will stop buying food! In true form, he sleeps everywhere — in the metro, on the busses, in the park, and if seated, in a museum. We both still are quite tired--around 5:00 p.m. we absolutely fade. Tonight we will go to sleep by 10:00 p.m. because we are getting up early, around 7:30, to take an English guided tour of Montparnasse. It is a 45-minute metro ride from here and will involve a lot of walking.

I am feeling a lot better about everything. The sun is out, we are making plans, and getting rest. On Monday I will go to a yoga class hopefully. C'est tout pour maintenant. A bientot!

May 13, 2001 — Sunday, 7:00 PM

Mother's Day in the states and I completely forgot this. We had a busy day. We awoke early to take the English guided tour of Montmartre, not Montparnasse. Saw Moulin Rouge, Place Pigalle, Sacre Coeur, and the homes at various times of Utrillo, Toulouse Lautrec, Renoir, Erik Satie (3 meters squared!) It was surprisingly nice to hear English and to explore with other Americans. Also saw the restaurant Le Lapin Agile. It is very famous and beautiful and old and I want to go there for dinner! Steve Martin wrote a play about it.

Observations about the metro: Sunday metro is very different than during the week; it is empty and eerie walking thru the long passageways with no music playing, very few people. Those in sight wore shorts and carried small suitcases. The weekend away I suspect. Yesterday on a very crowded metro a woman got on with a small old fashioned, heavy looking carriage containing a baby. On her back! was a large suitcase and another small suitcase in the rear of the carriage. She pushed her way on, knocking into everyone in sight and suddenly the wheel of the carriage got stuck in the space between the door and the metro station. She cursed like a sailor, people helped her, she thanked no one and was thoroughly obnoxious. She was maybe in her fifties and with a baby? Couldn't figure it out.

Tonight we are going to the Place de l'Opera to have a glass of wine at the café at the Rue De La Paix and watch the world go by and take a small walk there. It's the thing to do in Paris.

We are getting used to life here, but the food situation remains dim. There is no such thing as dietetic food, no low cal drinks or low cal anything. I shudder to look in the mirror. While on Place Pigalle, Peter said "Lets have French fries at the MacDonald's" I tasted one — it was great! Tomorrow I attempt yoga at a class at noon and we do some logistic stuff.

May 15, 2001 — Tuesday morning, 8:30 AM

I couldn't write in this diary last night - way too tired. Yesterday was awful, just awful. Completely frustrating. Everything went wrong. It rained and we set out to find my yoga class. We walked in circles for 45 minutes and I got angry and frustrated and never did find the class. This was disappointment #1. Later, we left the apartment around 2:30 pm with all sorts of good intentions. We started at American Express and we did get some good info there. Then we went to the Opera where a very rude ticket seller told me very unclearly (I had to go through the whole process again with another person) that the performance (San Francisco Ballet) was completely sold out and they didn't sell tickets for any other performances until two weeks before the showing. Then we took the metro to FNAC, a chain of electronic stuff stores that has a huge ticket service in its lower floor. We wanted to get tickets for something and there was nothing for us to buy. I still can't believe there isn't a concert, either of classical, jazz or other kind of music that I want to see. We were both disappointed.

All of a sudden, I cry out, "I'm falling!" Not amusing. People were simply walking around me. After reviving, we took a trip to an internet place on the Left Bank and Peter sat at the computer for 45 minutes. After that we found a little Japanese restaurant and had a so so meal of barbecued and skewered fish with rice, miso soup, a sauerkraut (?) salad and sake—the best part. After eating I was feeling more mellow and we luckily found a metro about a 5 minute walk away which took us back and Peter accidentally found an English speaking movie on TV. It was Canadian and had French subtitles; something I would never watch at home, but I am desperate for some TV or movies! DESPERATE. And so, I went to bed around 11:30 after reading a bit from my David Sedaris book. I really am addicted to media.

Friends, I can tell you that I am really starting to miss what we left behind. Probably because it is mostly inconvenient here. I was sorely disappointed about the yoga but will try again today. My body needs it so badly. Even with all the walking (and we walk MILES every day) I feel all bound up.

Peter said we were giving up our standard of living at home to be here and he is so right. No radio (except for music, thankfully), no TV really, no cars to whip around in, not the food we normally eat, and of course our apartment is nowhere as nice as the home we left behind. Since we sold the house before we left, our home is gone forever. It feels strange.

I actually cried yesterday from frustration. I don't feel lonely but it would be nice to speak to some other people. We are going to look into that today as there is a Jewish community center nearby. I would LOVE to have my car for a day. Traffic here is unbearable but to avoid those damn metro steps for just one day would be a blessing.

8:30 PM approximately

Yes, a better day. Mainly because we took it easier. I went to yoga this a.m. We found the yoga studio in ten minutes time, but boy! It is a miracle that we did as it is down an alley, behind a big black door, in a courtyard, a teeny place. The class was fine but too short, just an hour. I may go back tomorrow morning for a class that goes from 10:30 to noon. There are no early classes and these later classes really cut into the day. The teacher, M. Arnaund says to me "Parisians don't like getting up early for anything!" The class had six students in it including me. He watched me which was good because the entire class was in French and I needed his tutelage. Peter met me after and we had lunch at a place I FINALLY liked, a café (better than a brasserie) and I had a fabulous omelet that had in it potatoes, onions and mushrooms, along with a small green salad. This cost 44 francs or $6. Finally a good deal in a nice place. We got tickets for a gypsy music concert two weeks from now.

Took a short walk and then spent the rest of the day in the apartment working on the internet. I pushed Peter and now he is out playing basketball at a school gym about 10 metro stops from here. He should be back around 11:00 p.m. I hope! It's so difficult to get to do the things we take for granted at home; yoga, basketball, even getting tickets for events is a major deal. I wrote an email after he left and it will come to about $17 — too much — will cut this down to once every 2 weeks. I will do some paperwork regarding this trip, take a hot bath in some new Yves Rocher bath lotion I bought yesterday on the Champs-Elysees (where I fell) — and then some reading and dodo.

Love and xxx A BETTER ME

May 16, 2001 — Wednesday, 10 PM

A fun day. I went out this morning early in the slight drizzle and bought a Pariscope which is a weekly little magazine a la TV Guide that tells you all that is going on in Paris, the Herald Tribune for Peter, some tee shirts for him, and flowers for me. It was fun bopping from little shop to little shop in the rain and saying "Bonjour" to the trade's people.

Then, the logistics problems began anew. We attempted to do laundry in the washers and dryers in our building. It took about 3 hours and we ended up with two loads of wet laundry; this, for about $15. There has to be a better way. We later discovered a public economical laundromat nearby in the neighborhood. Plus going up and down up and down several times and the laundry room is in the very front of the building and we are in the very rear. After that, with tempers flaring (mostly mine) we headed out about 1:00 p.m. for Musee D'Orsay. A glorious place! So many French Impressionist works in a beautiful building that was a railroad station and still houses a huge waiting room clock. We were told it is the original clock. We stayed there until 5:30 p.m. We had an easy time of it getting there and back. I counted and we walked up 180 steps all told today. This was an EASY day! The exhibits were magnificent; almost too much so. How can one appreciate so much and see it all without getting a bit blasé? We went out on the terrasse, which overlooks the city, and it started to rain. We sat on a bench with the umbrella raised. It was wonderful, that is, until a lady came out and told us in no certain terms that the terrasse is ferme! I guess they don't want wet people trotting around the museum. We had a snack there and, as usual, it's so hard for us to eat out. We had cheese sandwiches for lack of anything better. All else was meat or fried stuff.

Dinner in our place and I appreciate the plain stuff. I made broiled salmon and steamed veggies. Afterwards, we folded the laundry which I had to strew all around the apartment to get it dry and then took a walk. We discovered upper Oberkampf, a really happening area, just steps away from our apartment. "I love this! the real non touristy Paris!" This from Peter.

Lots of restaurants and cafes and charming little boutiques among the doggy do. A lot of it.

Unfortunately, Peter and I got into a little to do or, as Judge Judy would say, a "kerfuffle." We found a shop that rents DVDs (movies in English) and I was ecstatic and wanted to rent one. Peter thought it was a bad idea as it was late and I wouldn't get to watch the whole thing and, as he put it, "I don't want to pay for two nights". This upset me as I don't want to watch every penny while we are here. It is enough that our standard of living is compromised. If I want to watch a movie over two nights and spend $7 instead of $3.50 so be it.

Peter has a different approach to this money stuff. It took some doing getting us here and I don't want to worry or think about every penny. He does. It is getting difficult for me. It's enough that my comfort level is lowered. But then again, he is a lot more rugged than I am!

Tomorrow we plan on going early to a cybercafé (I am getting sick of the internet for real) then to rue Buci for the outdoor market for some good food, and, maybe, going to rue Lafayette and visiting the Jewish Center.

Tomorrow night we will have dinner at an Italian restaurant we just discovered near here. I loved the museum today. Makes all the chaos we have to go through worthwhile.

May 17, 2001 — Thursday, 11:00 PM — I think

"Bitch!" A woman called me this today and she had good reason. We disembarked from the metro Odeon early this am, maybe 10:30. I asked her, in the rain, standing on the street, if she knew where rue Buci was. I asked her in French. She looked at me bewilderedly (is there such a word) and didn't say anything. I waited for something to come out of her mouth. She was Asian so I thought she would know French. I finally said to myself, under my breath, "if she didn't know where the street is why didn't she just say so?" That's when she looked at me and called me a bitch.

We attempted to go the Buci Market, reputedly the best food market in Paris but found it is only open on Sundays. Stupid me.

We had a nice petit dejeuner at Paul's and talked to a few people who spoke English. It was quite pleasant — nowhere special to go; just meandering. We took a short walk. The weather cooperated and then we headed uptown to the Bastille where we promptly found the cyber place Peter was looking for. I dropped him off and took off on my own to explore. Two different sets of people asked me for directions. In French. I answered them in French and felt empowered! I use "a gauche" and "a droit" a lot. Left and right. And straight ahead is "tout droit". We then (after Peter was there almost two hours) ambled our way up Boulevard Bastille and lo and behold! a health food store or reasonable facsimile thereof. NOTHING compared to what we have here, not even close, but we got some vegetarian "meat" and tahini. I am thrilled. We then got tickets to a one-woman performance tomorrow night at the Theatre Bastille. I think she is a Spanish dancer.

About peeing I must say a word or two. We have changed our bathroom habits completely. No longer can we wait until we have to go, because where would there be a bathroom for sure? So now we go wherever we find a toilette, whether the urge is there or not. So, in every restaurant and at the cyber cafés, we go. Also we cannot drink as much water as we are accustomed to. I drank a lot today, and a big cup of coffee this a.m., and have been going all evening. Sometimes I worry about this stuff. How many times is too many?

I think I know why so many Parisians (if not all of them) have cell phones. Because they are never home. They are either at work, at play, or at a café. We had dinner at a cute little Italian restaurant, and when we left at 9:30 people were just starting to come in. How do they do it — stay up late and then go to work the next day? We are baffled.

Tried to rent a DVD afterwards and by the time we got there at 10 p.m. the store was closed! Am I fated never to see a movie while I am in Paris? Tomorrow I MUST find a manicurist. My acrylics are in terrible shape, too long, one thumb has turned black (fungus or injury underneath) and the acrylic on the other thumb is completely off, something I've never experienced. It is fantastic to me that there are no nail places. We've been all over the place and I only found one manicure parlor and the woman who does acrylic nails won't be back for ten days — she is on vacation! One woman in the whole place does fills. She should visit the Valley. She would clean up. Also, Peter needs to have his shoes repaired. I will go back to the local yoga. It's not the best but convenient and I did get a good workout on Tuesday. C'est tout.

Hurrah for Hollywood! It's Friday night and on our way to the Theatre Bastille we found a manicurist! And a synagogue! Right now the manicurist has more meaning for me . It seems that she won't be in until Wednesday. Also, there is one across the street who won't be in until Monday. It is astonishing to me that the shop would have one manicurist who only works part time. I think of L.A. and the fact that there are usually four manicure salons on a block.

Today we piddled around the apartment and left around 1:00 to find the Jewish Community Center. Got some information about their events but I think Peter wanted more of a community getting together English-speaking Jews kind of thing. Does this exist? We went to Galleries Lafayette afterwards where we had salads in its newly remodeled cafeteria. I like the old one better. It had more charm. This store is still amazing — the ceiling — its dome — all the glass — and the store itself is magnificent — large and modern with so much merchandise. Peter camped out on a red plush chair with his paper while I searched through purses. There must be 1,000 different styles. I felt too much pressure and will have to return on my own.

May 19, 2001 — Saturday, 10:30 AM

Peter is out jogging. I will go to yoga at 12:30 (these classes are so late) and later we will go to Montparnasse for the day and evening. We are taking things a bit slower now. The frenzy to get out early and stay out until we are completely wiped out is over. We know we have time to do it all. So be it.

There are the same frustrations, even after resigning ourselves to the fact that the things we take so for granted are just not available to us. We are better about it all. I am having trouble getting on the internet. I wanted to read my emails at leisure while Peter was out, but I can't gain access. Also, I want to sit and make a phone call from the room to a friend back home. At the cost of 2 francs or 14 cents a minute Peter says no, wait until we can use the phone card in a phone booth. I feel this is a bit too penurious on his part.

So what if it costs a few bucks, we are not paying a phone bill at home. I find I need a measuring cup, electrical tape and matches. Good luck. If we were in the heart of Paris this would be easy because more people speak English, here, well, it will be trial and error. The charm, after a while, of their not being able to speak English, wears thin. Am I becoming an ugly American? Hope not.

I had yoga, piano, the museum, my friends and, for almost a year, getting ready for this trip which took a lot of time and energy. That is all done now, and it is supposed to be nothing but fun and games. Not sure I like just fun and games.

It is a beautiful sunny day but I don't trust this! The rain could start coming down any minute now. Peter says "Let's be optimistic and go out without an umbrella." The shlepping gets annoying, too. How convenient having a car is! Will have some breakfast now and watch CNN. Love to the Valley.

11:00 PM

A splendid day. Went to a "detente" yoga class at 12:30 which turned out to be 75% restoratives. I felt punky so this was a good thing for me. The class is only an hour long but feels longer. During the restorative portion while we were relaxing M. Arnaud did the meditation in French. I did not understand much so I kind of just hung out with it. I committed to ten hours, so I will take some more active classes, hopefully at more convenient times. And he holds classes in the evening also.

In the afternoon, Peter mapped out our day at Montparnasse. He did a good job and got us there by metro after which we started the walking tour as outlined in Fodor's. We promptly went the wrong way but corrected ourselves. We went up the Tour Montparnasse, the tallest building in Western Europe which has 59 floors, an outside terrace and we saw all of Paris — quite an amazing sight — Paris is truly a gorgeous city in every way. We walked a bit in this very crowded area that had lots of movie houses but only one or two American films, which we had already seen. Had dinner in the area at a very charming little restaurant. And soon to bed and the New Yorker. Tomorrow we go to the Richard Lenoir Street market in the a.m. and maybe the Paris jazz festival in the afternoon into evening. We sound so busy.

May 20, 2001 — Sunday, 7 PM

Today we went to a GREAT open air food market at Port Aligre which is an Arab section. It was maybe a half of a mile or longer, with stalls on both sides of the street, vendors hawking their wares, incredibly wonderful vegetables and fruit; things I haven't seen ever, huge bulbs of garlic on very long thick stems, gigantic red tomatoes and more. Bought more flowers and veggies and fruit and came home. I took a very hot bath (my back hurt from the yoga as well as my knees — I don't know what I did but it wasn't good), had a little cereal with a bunch of vitamins and went to bed. Stayed there until about 4 pm.

We went out, got the DVDs and then I packed a picnic, which we took to a local park which proved to be another not so short walk. We stayed there a few hours and I am back now, not watching the movies I rented. Will clean up the apartment AGAIN and put away my clothes and read a little, map out some plans for the week, get to bed early. As Scarlett would say, "Tomorrow is another day. Fiddle de de."

May 21, 2001 — Monday, 10:30 PM

Today was really nice. So many of our days are. We went to the cybercafé together, I did my thing, left Peter and proceeded to rue Royal and the shops on rue Faubourg St. Honore. First metro I took alone this trip. I dressed up a little and it was very nice to be on a street with lovely shops and well-dressed people. I ambled a bit and came upon the purse store where I bought a purse a few years ago. I am up for another one and almost got it, but didn't. Had lunch at a brasserie/café in a courtyard in Rue Royal. Most chic. One gets on line indoors and wine is passed, free. You place your order, find a seat, and then the food is brought to you. I sat alone and two gentlemen sat next to me. The seats are very close to each other. It was interesting because they were watching me closely and I liked it! An older woman came and sat down across the very narrow aisle from me and she was well known; the owner came out and kissed her on both cheeks. She was dressed beautifully. I admired her élan.

Took the metro to Georg V stop on the Champs-Elysees and met Peter. We proceeded to a movie house on this Boulevard and were going to see "Finding Forrester." We were told it wasn't playing there anymore but was playing further down the block. Okay. Went THERE and "Finding Forrester" was playing there all right, but in French. It plays in English only twice a day, early in the a.m. and late in the p.m. We went in to a movie anyway. I had to see a movie, and saw "A Few Good Men". It was better than I thought but highly predictable. My first movie in Paris. A good rest also as the theater showed lots and lots of ads not only for upcoming movies but also for products, sodas and perfume and lots more. Maybe 20-25 minutes of ads before the movie came on.

After, we ambled a bit as the weather is fabulous; sunny and warm and no need for a sweater. Purchased two tee shirts We walked more and ended up in Les Halles! I wanted to go there one day anyway. Most of the streets are closed to traffic and you walk as if on a promenade. We had Chinese food at a little place and it was very good and quite reasonable. And then on to the metro and we are back in our little home.

Observations — everyone is outdoors. Eight million people in Paris and they are all out at cafes. It is amazing how many people you see on the streets and in cars. Lunchtime, a lot of people buy sandwiches of jambon and fromage in baguettes and eat them while walking down the street. I tell Peter maybe that's the secret of staying thin. Tomorrow, Bercy. Bonne Nuit.

May 22, 2001 — Tuesday, 8:00 PM — Still sunny and warm

Well, I've done it. I have the most god-awful head cold complete with runny nose, congestion, phlegm (I'm pretty sure that's how you spell it) and very fatigued. Pissed off. Sick in Paris. Bummer times 100. Peter has gone to play basketball and I'm glad that he won't have to deal with me for a while!

I have on a documentary on "Best in Show" in Italian. It features an interview with Eugene Levy who wrote it and is in it. I see his face with Italian words coming out of his mouth. I phoned Ronni a bit ago and it was 8:30 a.m. She said Howard Stern was on the radio. I could use a bit of Howard. I'm desperate. She was so excited to hear from me. It is just amazing how we are connected in a matter of seconds and we hear each other as if we were in the same room. I tried phoning my brother, my cousin and a friend, but they are not in. Will try in a few days.

Today was nice. We took the bus to Bercy part of the way and ended up doing the final stretch on the metro and vowed to stay off the metro for at least a day to no avail. Bercy is great, urban renewal to the umph degree. Very gentrified. We followed up with a visit to La Bibliotheque Francaise, which is four buildings about 20 stories and houses over eleven million books! We walked around a bit indoors at one of the buildings and had lunch at the cafeteria.

Mes amis, we don't know nuthin' about good food. The French have it over us by volumes. Even a pre-made, pre-wrapped veggie sandwich is fresh and delicious. Is it possible to have a bad meal in France? I think not. I think the museums and schools must get all of their sandwiches from one place because they are all wrapped the same, and very nicely done. Going to get my tea now and am going to drink a barrel of it. Maybe it'll help with my cold.

We went to a pharmacy nearby to get some cold stuff and when we asked the pharmacist if he spoke English he said "a little" but that he spoke Hebrew! Guess he knew we were Jewish. We asked him for the name of a Reform synagogue and we may go Friday night. It is in the Victor Hugo section, which is quite upscale.

Peter and I took a bus all around the Left Bank and had no clue where we were going. We came upon the famous cemetery in Montparnasse that was closed on Sunday. We walked through but couldn't find any well-known people although a lot are buried there. It's very old and some of the tombs are like little houses. Doesn't hold a candle to Pere Lachaisse Cemetery, in my opinion.

May 23, 2001 — Wednesday, 8:00 PM

Well ladies and gentlemen, boys and girls, one and all, I am tres malade and it's a drag. To be in Paris and feel sick as a dog and have to stay put — ooh la la —ain't fun. And historically, it seems that my colds last forever.

Nevertheless, went out this a.m. and had my nails done — nothing was going to stop that! She did a fabulous job and it was expensive, 275 francs with the tip but it is 30 francs more than it had to be due to the fact that she had to put on my thumbnails. After, we did some errands. We meandered our way to the Champs Elysees to exchange some travelers checks for francs and got a very good rate —7.40 — the dollar is very strong now. Peter is happy. We then went to the American Express to take care of more business. Stopped at Brentano's and bought a book to share; short stories by authors all over the globe. We then sat on the steps of l'Opera — a great thing to-do — what a view! All the gorgeous avenues laying at our feet. Went to Rue Faubourg St-Honore and got the red purse I liked. Peter liked it better in black. C'est la vie. I love it and will use is immediately.

As I was fading fast, got back to the rooms around 4:00 pm and attempted to sleep but the mind was too active. Peter made phone calls. I tried to make phone calls and got no one in, guess I'll have to time it better. Tomorrow we go and do emails.

Some thoughts. I am writing this while slightly but only slightly drunk, dirty dishes waiting to be done, Peter took a walk. I want to do it all and see it all. Not possible. I'd kill for anything in English on TV right now. CNN is such a boring drag. The same news over and over again. Where is Larry King now that I need him anyway?

I'm finally so happy to be here, sick as I am. The weather is divine — sunny and about 80 degrees today. Just walking around Paris is pure joy. I am going to peruse Pariscope and figure out stuff to do.

Sometimes just doing nothing is great, but then I think — PARIS. Must do it all, see it all. Silly me. Have you ever taken a bunch of vitamin pills with wine? I just did — feels great. Going to write a post card or two, then take a very hot bath and hopefully, dodo.

And how was YOUR day, mon amie? Bonne Nuit.

May 24, 2001 — Thursday, 11 PM — Ascension Day

We were out until just a few minutes ago. Woke up today with no voice, but it came back during the day. I am taking everything I can to rid myself of this. Tres fatigue. Still, we persevere.

Went on a tour of the Marais' "hotels" (not really hotels at all — government buildings) in French. A big mistake. Didn't get much out of it. Peter was mad at me for doing this. Now we know, only English-speaking tours. However, did get a nice walk and had lunch at La Turenne in the Marais — quite good and a front row view of the street — does anybody eat indoors in Paris, I wonder? Maybe they should build restaurants completely outdoors except for the kitchens. Walked from there to the Bastille where we both did our thing with emails. Hated it there today — hot and dusty and no air conditioner. An omen of things to come as we get more and more into Summer? And, in the end, Peter has to go back in the a.m. to do more emails. I will not be going with him, that's for sure! Got back to the apartment, collapsed onto the couch and lay there for a few hours, took a very hot bath and then Peter and I had dinner. I had tea and toast which was all I wanted. Decided to go out in the evening for a bit and so we went to Pont Alma to get a Bateau Mouche. It was a wonderful one hour's boat ride.

Paris is gorgeous anytime, but sitting on a boat going up and down the Seine was sublime. Then the city of lights went dark. We passed the Tour d'Eiffel which was all lit up and on the stroke of 10 p.m. sparkling lights from every part of it descended upon us.

We viewed some amazing sights. By the Ile de Cite, on the shore there were young people doing what looked like square dancing, there was huge crowds of people walking and sitting by the Seine, musicians playing, and of course, all the lit up historical buildings along the way. I think Parisians have been holed up all winter because of the dreadful weather they had, and now that it is nice, out they come. The cafes on the streets are full of people. Don't these people have to get up early to go to work? I wonder how they manage this.

Tomorrow I will feel good — I am DETERMINED. A bientot.

May 25, 2001 — Friday, 8:30 PM

I wasn't going to write anything today because it's been kind of a blah day, but Peter says that would set a precedent, so here I am, writing. I feel a little bit better today. Went out late in the a.m. to the rue Faubourg St-Honore and walked among the chic boutiques. Who buys these clothes anyway? Mostly highly unwearable. I met Peter at his new cyber cafe and then we did some errands. We got tickets for the Garnier Opera House, to see a ballet. It's such a beautiful venue! I am really looking forward to this. Then, we spent about three hours on busses wandering around and ended up in the suburbs of Paris which was so boring to behold that all we did is get off the bus at the last stop and then get on again to return to Paris proper. We had a bite and a beer at a local cafe on Oberkampf. I like the area — it is very happening and also very young. Now, I will prepare for bed and maybe read a little. We want to have lights out by ten. We have to get up around 6 a.m. as tomorrow is our all-day excursion to the Loire Valley. This is a good test for me to see if I like an all-day trip, or, would rather break it up by sleeping in a hotel and taking two days. Bon Nuit, y'all.

May 27, 2001 — Sunday, 1:30 PM — La fete de mere (Mother's Day) here

I am in a foul mood. Couldn't do this diary last night because I was just too tired. We took a twelve hour trip through the Loire Valley and viewed the chateaux and small towns and the Loire River. Arose at 6 a.m. to meet with the bus at 7:45 a.m. The tour was great but very long on the bus; hours and hours. We saw amazing places and beautiful little provincial towns. It was all quite charming and I especially like the Chateau Chenonceau — very lovely, moat, water, huge gardens et al. When we returned to the Trocadero area, we did some walking and around 10 p.m. decided to return to the apartment since we were tired. Well, folks. The metro on Saturday night from L'Etoile is a mess. We had to change three times, walk a great deal, both flat and up and down lots of flights of stairs. I was angry at this. Why can't we take a cab once in a while? He thinks we are in our twenties and poor. He loves to spend money, however, on food. Not food in restaurants, but in the markets. Loves to market.

Today we wait for Xavier and Corinne to pick us up and we are going to Bois de Vincennes for a picnic and to hear some jazz. On our very first trip to Paris, we stayed in Vincennes which is a small town about an hour outside of Paris. Thank goodness they are picking us up by car.

I told Peter I want to go out at night. I need to see nice-looking well-dressed people in great places. What's wrong with that anyway? I guess I am always pissed at heart that he doesn't feel the same way.

May 28, 2001 — Monday, 10:00 PM

Hot hot hot! Sticky humid hot in the apartment. I didn't write yesterday's doings because I was very tired and I had terribly irritated eyes due to the smog and the fact that I had sun tan oil on my hands and then rubbed my eyes. Ouch.

Yesterday we didn't go out (except for early a.m. errands) until later afternoon. Xavier and Corinne picked us up and we went to the Parc Floral in the Bois de Vincennes to hear a jazz concert. The group was the Russell Malone quartet. Russell plays for Diane Krall.

They were FABULOUS. We sat on the lawn behind the stage as we were too late to get seats, but after a while we did get seats as some people left and we were right there to get them. The park is gorgeous and aptly named — all flowers, in different areas, different types, huge and colorful. I felt like I was in Central Park because it had the same kind of active-people feel and not at all like the park in Woodland Hills which is where we lived. We had a picnic but no one else picnicked.

Today is Monday and we went to the Pompidou Museum. We saw various exhibits, one excellent temporary one on pop art, not just USA but France as well. Had lunch al fresco on the 6th floor overlooking the entire city. Paris does not have many tall buildings so if you are on the 6th floor you see most of Paris rooftops and parks, etc. After beaucoup hours there we walked to Ile de Cite where we ambled around and went into Notre Dame, which has been sandblasted on the exterior and looks so beautiful. You can see the statuary in all their glory. Walked further into the Left Bank where Peter paid $50 for a pair of sunglasses. "I'm desperate," he says. It is very hot and very sunny and painful without the proper gear.

Took the metro to our area and dinner at a Chinese restaurant by accident. We were heading for another restaurant, got lost (natch) but found this really good one. Some French youths at the next table spoke to us not realizing we were American. I did really well for a while! Mais oui!

I must say that the Parisians are the nicest people I've ever met — vraiment! They go out of their way to help you — in so many ways, so many examples, they have been so thoughtful of us poor aliens. A bientot.

June 2001, EUROPE

Le 7 Juin 2001 — Jeudi, 1:30 PM

Sitting at a cafe in the Louvre and will meet Peter at 3 pm here. I wanted to be definite about what I want to see (the desire to write in shorthand is huge but since I can't type this out on the computer I don't trust myself to read it back later on!)

Chocolat chaud et un verre d'eau. This is the dejeuner today. I wanted to see the crown jewels, l'histoire de Louvre, Napoleon's apartments and 19° century French paintings — all closed on Thursdays! I Was told there's an English-speaking tour of something at 2:00 p.m., but with my luck, who knows? The desire to write is strong and I see now it must be in handwriting, so I bought this notebook since the other two are in the apartment. I shall have a collection of museum notebooks!

In Peter's pile of sweaters, I found my grey cashmere. I was delighted because I thought I left it home and guess what? Moth holes in the turtleneck! Merde!

This whole Paris deal is surreal to me — am I really here? Am I really at the Louvre, surrounded by vast amounts of incredible art from all ages? Or is it a fantastically wild dream?

I walked several flights of stairs here and my heart was beating madly — should I worry about this? And my eyes; without glasses life is a blur. Richard Gere could walk by and I wouldn't know it. Do you think Richard Gere comes here? Are there any movie stars in Paris? I'm sure there are, but certainly not in my neighborhood.

I shall put on my best black clothes and saunter to a few chic hotels, sans Peter! And in sunglasses, natch. Going to finish my chocolat and meander. Can't waste a minute.

3:33 PM

Three minutes late to meet Peter. I just came from seeing Mona. I walked what seemed several miles up lots of stairs, down a very, very long hallway, past magnificent Italian paintings, just giving them a glance on the road to see Mona, and does she appreciate this?

Mona Lisa or to use her formal name La Gioconda, is under glass, on her very own wall with a strong iron bar about six feet around her. I got up front, past hundreds of people snapping photos (they can now prove to everyone back home that they've "seen" her) and stood here a full five minutes gazing. "I want to spend more time with you," I tell Mona. I can really understand why she is the most famous painting in the world.

I saw Mona a few times, the first being when I was in my twenties and came to Paris on my own. At that time, she was the last on a wall with other paintings, no glass, and no barriers, just a single guard. You could get really close to her then. She is beautiful and her expression wonderous, defying explanation. Mona is serene and earthy at the same time. She is my heroine and I can't explain why. I'd like to see more of her. In fact, I'd like to take her to tea. Or for a glass of wine.

I bought a little change purse in a shop in the "Carousel" (mall) of the Louvre. The price in the window said 89 francs but the proprietor charged me 9 gf. I showed her the window and she said that it was an error. I must have looked annoyed because, of course, she should have sold it to me for the quoted price, so she gave me a postcard of my choice and that is how I got my lovely little picture of Mona Lisa.

June 8, 2001 — Friday night, 11:30 PM

Had the most splendiferous time tonight. We went to the Opera Garnier to see the ballet. If I just sat in my red velvet chair and looked all around me at the Chagall ceiling, the magnificent chandelier (shades of Phantom of the Opera!), the beautiful gold boxes, all the marble, sculptures and paintings, it would have been more than enough. And, the wonderous, wonderful ballet was too magnificent for words. Am so glad that we purchased the program for $7.00, because it has pictures and describes each of the eight ballets, albeit in French. Afterwards, we went to a Cafe at Rue de la Paix, but had to sit inside due to the cold weather. It was a bit disappointing — such a famous place always filled with lots of people in good weather, kind of empty. Oh well — c'est la vie.

We had "cacher" pasta with Sidney today. He is one of a kind; Peter's friend from American Express. We are having Sabbath dinner at his house next week. Yes, Peter made what turned out to be a lifelong friend at American Express.

Attended the fashion show at Galleries Lafayette today. So so — not haute couture. All kinds of playful casual clothes with not much zing to them; no big deal.

Each day when we enter the metro there are musicians playing for handouts. While waiting for our train the opposite train came by and we could see and hear a trumpet and a tuba. Yesterday we heard a violinist playing Hava Nagila. I will probably have to stay up and read or watch TV until I sober up. This is so strange. I'm tired but I don't dare close my eyes and I think I feel heartburn coming but maybe not. Shabat Shalom.

June 9, 2001 — Saturday, 9:00 PM

I am sitting in my robe, on the couch next to Peter listening to my new Russell Malone CD. He is jazz guitarist we saw two weeks ago at Vincennes Jazz Festival.

Werner from the Mayflower Hotel met us for lunch today. "Hi again, Werner." Went to a strange restaurant on the 6th floor of an office building. There was no way to tell that there was a large, open-air restaurant inside. Had an expensive and stupid lunch. It was a salad that was supposed to have seven kinds of vegetables and turned out to have seven kinds of lettuce with tiny cherry tomatoes. Had to get a side order of fromage, dessert and cafe. We had a lovely view of the Eiffel Tower which is on the Left Bank. Werner is sweet, smart and very unassuming. We walked on the Champs Elysees with him until 4:00 PM.

Spent the rest of the day walking and went back to the apartment early, around 6:30. The Parisians and tourists are out in full force on this sunny day. We walked Avenue Montaigne and saw all the high fashions shops. The Japanese ladies are lined up outside the Vuitton shop on the Champs Elysees. They love LV! Tomorrow we meet Marjorie's friend Joan for lunch in Montmartre.

June 10, 2001 — Sunday, 10:00 PM

Time is starting to fly. It feels like I wrote in this book just a minute ago and it was 24 hours. Last night was kind of a lousy night, for want of a better word. I was feeling tired and spacey and fell asleep around 11:00 PM. The phone rang at 1:00 p.m. and I awoke with the start —it was a business call for Peter for an hour. I couldn't get back to sleep and was furious with Peter. He told the man on the other end that it was ok to call at that hour. I finally fell asleep after taking a pill and we didn't get out of bed until around 10:00 this morning.

We left for Montmartre and met Joan, Marjorie's good friend, at the Place du Tertre at 12:45. It was mobbed. We had lunch at a large outdoor restaurant right in the middle of the Place called La Mere Catherine. It was a wonderful atmospheric spot, surrounded by lots of artists, some wanting to do sketches of us. Our lunch was good and I am eating so much "bad" stuff, which tastes so divine. But I am never really full; small portions and high prices.

We walked to one of the last remaining, and maybe the smallest vineyards in Paris right across the street from Au Lapin Agile. It was a special event in that all the vineyards in Paris were open today and you could tour them and drink the wine for l0 francs. The weather turned nasty — windy, cold and a few drops of rain fell. We hurried to the metro. Joan stayed on and we returned to our place to rest a bit and change. Then, a 6:00 p.m. movie in a strange tiny theatre near the Bastille. There was less than 10 people (there were three screens in all). We saw "Basquiat" which was a gem of a movie, actually a great film about the graffiti artist who dies of an overdose of heroin at the age of 27. Walked backed in sunshine to our place and had some food. Tomorrow will be an errand day and Tuesday we leave for Dijon.

Observation. There is so much I can say about Paris. This is a place of dreams and fantasy. It's so perfect despite the inconveniences. Or maybe I am just becoming more adaptable. The buildings, the art, the music, the greenery, the promenades, the shops, the cafes, the food, always the food, the streets, the gentility of it all, the caring of the people of their surroundings, the reverence of preserving the old and beautiful, the grace, the warmth, not caring about the last dollar, and so much more is what brings about the state of mind that Paris produces. I feel so fortunate to be able to partake and breathe all this into my body and spirit. This is truly a dream I want to keep on dreaming.

June 11, 2001 — Monday, 9:45 PM

Still bright out. Even at this hour. Eventful day — quelle surprise! Went outside of Paris to a Toshiba repair place with our laptop. Took our first RER train to a town I can't pronounce too far away. Arrived lunch time so all was closed, but of course! Forged ahead to a local cafe and had an excellent salad. The owner waited on us and tried so hard to please. Everyone in it, and it was packed, was eating gigantic portions of steak and fries and beer, dessert and coffee. Lots of businessmen. The area was decidedly industrial. It was a hoot. We returned a few hours later after getting some help at Toshiba and I went to the cyber cafe solo; so much better without Peter breathing down my neck. I went to a local cafe and had a super duper ice cream sundae with chocolate and liquor sauce and read USA today. Back to the apartment, had dinner and packed for our trip. And now to bed.

Le 12 Juin 2001 — Mardi, 2:45 PM Tuesday

On our way to Dijon. We are sitting at the Hertz Car Rental place waiting for a car, which should be here at 3:00. After a train ride of 97 minutes, we arrived at Dijon precisely at 10:21 a.m.— the total miles from Paris to Dijon is 193 miles. We took the TVG from Gare de Lyon and traveled at a very fast speed. The train was fabulous plus the seats had a nice table between us (we sat opposite each other in single seats). The countryside rolled by and Peter dozed off while I had the cafe du lait I bought at the station. We walked forever on the platform to the train. We had reserved seats in first class, which made the walk worthwhile. A couple and their college age son just came in only to find that there is no car for them — and they reserved from Kansas City! Ooh la la!

10:00 PM Beaune. A city in Burgundy

This by far is one of the weirder experiences we have had traveling. I am sitting on a bed in a room about twice as large as our apartment in Paris, maybe 700 to 800 feet. It is in a hotel that used to be an Abbaye and was built in the 15 Century. The cave, yes cave, that serves as its restaurant was built in the 7th Century. It is amazing to behold and we are going to have breakfast in it tomorrow morning.

I feel like a princess in a castle that is very medieval and stony with huge windows at least 20 feet high floor to ceiling at that. We rented this room through the tourist office in town. We drove down from Dijon through vineyards and open fields and fleetingly saw a chateau or two. I say fleetingly because the single lane road didn't allow us to drive slowly with lots of cars and trucks speeding along behind and in front of us. We have a cute tiny Ford with stick shift and Peter took right to it. I navigate and he drives.

Beaune is a wine drinker's paradise with lots of "caves" and tasting rooms and with many pretty and expensive shops and brasseries. One can walk the entire town in an hour and see magnificent old churches and buildings everywhere. For an Abbaye the surrounding streets aren't very quiet.

June 13, 2001 — Wednesday, 9:30 AM

Just got back from breakfast. Sat against a wall that is 1700 years old! It is one of the original walls that enclosed the city of Beaune. Eating in the cave was a fantastic experience. Spoke with the owner who told us about the small wine growers in the area. He says there's a town named Parents. This town is a few buildings inside a vineyard that has been growing grapes for a thousand years and owned by the same family which is about 50 generations! Est-ce que possible? We will tour this town and the famous hospital and then drive to and through the small town later.

9:45 PM

We are in a lovely and charming hotel in a town called Autun, which is in the southwest area of France, about an hour's drive from Dijon if you drive the straight route. We didn't, we drove south and then west from Beaune. We left Beaune about 2:00 pm having spent the morning there. We had lunch at a very large cafeteria in a new mall, which Peter found while walking this morning. Peter really likes cafeterias. It was such culture shock after being in medieval towns to find this in the outskirts of Beaune. In this mall was a huge supermarche where we bought fruit, water and chocolate. We drove to a town called Pommard. I fell in love with it. The few hundred people who live there all own wineries and work the surrounding vineyards, which have been in their families for hundreds of years. It is a rich town, completely walkable in an hour. It consists of two or three small shops, a large eglise, the "maire" and a large chateau now a winery.

We stopped at a cave, which you had to see by ringing the bell of a lovely house. The owner, a jolly fat provincial lady opened the eave for us, which was underground and delightfully cool. We tasted and bought a bottle at 137 francs. She spoke no English but was well acquainted with "la Carte de credit!" I was absolutely thrilled with this encounter. It was charming and touched my spirit. After leaving this enchanting old town, we drove for three hours or so through several small towns, vineyards galore, fields of green and decided to stop here at Autun for the night. The hotel is called Ursulines and sits high on top the city adjacent to a magnificent cathedral. Our room overlooks a large lawn with some tables and beyond that, the countryside and the town.

We had a small dinner at a local Italian restaurant we came upon walking into the town. Tomorrow we will look at the many sights, which include a 2,000-year-old ruin of a Roman amphitheater, and a Mac Donald's. Ciao for now. Peter is watching TV in French. Desperate measures.

June 14, 2001 — Thursday, precisely 10:20 PM

We are on the TGV from Dijon going back to Paris and it leaves exactly on time. I don't know what to make of today. It was difficult. I awoke early this morning after a mostly sleepless night. We took off around 10:00 am to see the sights of Autun. Got lost. Didn't care. Decided to forego the ancient ruins and head toward Dijon the scenic way, little towns, farms, and chateaux. Got lost. Saw a sweet little rich town, not medieval about a half-hour west of Autun. Tried to find a road to Dijon. Got lost. We are back in Autun. Got directions and we're out of here, on our way to Dijon. Lots of big trucks and impatient cars on our rear. Not able to sight see; have to drive fast. Arrived at Dijon and to make an aggravating story short, it was a nightmare trying to find la gare (train station) and the Hertz car rental place.

After the help of a nice young man who led us the whole way there in his car, got lost one more time trying to find a gas station. Took us about an hour and we returned the car almost just in time. With just a few minutes to spare, Peter parked himself on a bench in a park and I went down the main drag to shop. Got some Dijon mustard for 12 francs each, five jars that were very heavy. Plan on taking a cab from Gare Lyon. Our bags are now heavy and we are tired. Right now the splendors of Burgundy escape me. Tomorrow I will recall it all.

June 16, 2001 — Saturday, 12:30

June 15

June 16, 2001 –- Saturday

I am having cafe du lait along with the croissant I bought at our patisserie, in a small and very unpretentious coffee/bar. Can you imagine bringing food from one place and sitting down with it in another place in the United States?

We are doing laundry and while the machines are churning Peter is jogging and I am here at a café across from the laundromat. I had so many emotions at this time. I love being here. I am homesick. I am homesick. I love being here.

Last night we had an incredible and wonderful experience that I'm sure few tourists have. We went to a Shabat dinner at the home of Sidney Belma, the gentleman we met at American Express. He, his wife Annette, daughter Caroline age 22 and son Jeremy age 21 live in a high-rise on the 7th floor in the suburbs of Paris. There is so much to tell about this evening!

The home has three bedrooms, one bath, living and dining room combo, small kitchen, small hallway and terrace. All the rooms by US standards would be considered tiny. They live together here quite happily and not too long ago two older sons lived here as well. Everyone shares the three small bedrooms. And one bathroom. Have to check the laundry.

The laundry is now safely ensconced in a large dryer. I am watching the total integration of blacks with whites, greens with greys. No pastels. I will wash the few colored shirts we have by hand. The automatic money taker for the dryer only takes 3 francs for 6 minutes at a time, which means I have to sit here.

Back to the Belma's. The table was set for Shabbat with candles, challeh, several European salads and wine. Peter was given a yarmalke and we all, including Annette's brother who is visiting, sat down and recited the prayers. Peter read from the bible with Sidney. We all sang Shabbat songs which I found I actually knew. It was so beautiful I wanted to cry.

The special food prepared for us being vegetarians, was served by Annette. It was very time consuming to create this meal which consisted of fish and couscous and kafteh and things I never ate before. We had tea and the exotic "cacher" desserts we bought earlier that day in the Jewish section on rue Montmartre, not to be confused with the Sacre Coeur area called Montmartre. Lots of stories were told and Annette's brother played the piano.

The two young adults are very, very remarkable. They were courteous and kind to us seemingly interested in all we had so say. They stayed with us at the table the entire evening. Caroline, the daughter, observed the Shabbat and would not use the camera because of this. I took pictures of everyone. Jeremy, the

21-year-old son, who is astonishingly handsome, drove us back to our apartment. This is a good 45-minute drive and he was very nice about it. Both have spent time in California. Jeremy just returned after being there a year so he is well acquainted with our lifestyle. He thinks Americans are very materialistic and he speaks of this very matter of factly, with no judgement. Where he does show his scorn is in the fact that the Americans he spoke with don't know anything about the politics of Europe and indeed don't even know where Tunisia is, the land of his father. He thinks rich people need to show their wealth by having big houses, cars, etc. Of course, this may be because he spent most of his time in Los Angeles!

It's about 11:00 pm. We finished the laundry, made two trips to supermarches, had a bite in the room and returned from the movies. Saw "Avant La Nuit" by Schnabel who did "Basquiat" which we saw last week. Another winner, but very sad, depressing and hapless. It was raining when we got out, but we walked from Republique after a stop a "Mc Do's". I told Peter "I am going to make reservations at least at two nice restaurants next week. I need to eat better and will just ask them to make the food sans everything!"

After seeing this movie, about the Cuban anti-revolutionary poet and writer Renaildo Arenas, I feel so inadequate in my writing. Do I have in me to write something meaningful or "this is my life stuff." I think I have stuff in me — but maybe it's just stuffing.

10:45 PM Sunday, Father's Day. Nothing from the kids that makes me sad and angry for Peter.

Just returned from having a bowl of pate et une verre de vin. Peter had a pizza. I spoke French with a young couple sitting next to us -- tres amusant.

Had breakfast at Paul's on the Left Bank near rue Buci with Xavier. "I like this place a lot" – this from Peter. You get a dejeuner complete (juice, eggs, hot drink, bread, confiture et beurre). We sat and talked and ate and then took a walk through the Luxembourg Gardens. It rained. We walked. It rained. We walked. It stopped raining. We walked through the streets to the Seine, over a bridge and into the Tuilleries. Gusty and windy — we came back to the apartment at 4:00 p.m. and rested. And so you have our days, they are flying by. Tomorrow we each go out solo. A good thing, but not the best day for me to do this as the museums and other attractions are closed on Lundi. Must do some grunge telephone calls, nails, hair, and reservations.

A few weeks into our trip we decided we needed time away from each other. We are together 24/7. Tuesdays would be good as, for me, I would go to a museum maybe and they are all open on Tuesdays. The rules is there is no rule; we go our own way and then join up in the evening. That way we could share our experiences of the day. Or not.

How we got to meet the Belma's. Peter and I met Sidney Belma at the American Express office at Place de l'Opera. We needed some logistic help and he was the man to ask, sitting on a stool, smack in the middle of the office, surrounded by a large circular high countered desk.

Peter and he got to talking and Peter asked him if he knew of any synagogues and this man became extremely excited! Turns out he is a religious Jew, originally from Tunisia. He is very animated and exuberant. Lots of energy. Peter and he talked for several minutes, but he would stop when someone needed some information; where to cash traveler's checks, how to get to a certain restaurant, what metro could take you to a certain place, what time a certain museum opened, which is the best city tour, and on and on. He would eagerly give each person his full attention and was very friendly with them and everyone left beaming. Then he would turn back to Peter and give him his full attention. This is the most joyful man I met. Think of it; he got instant and complete gratification from everyone he spoke with all day long. And he just loves his job. He is warm and caring and there is no question that he deemed stupid or inconsequential.

Sydney has worked for American Express for 38 years and will retire in a few months when he becomes sixty. It is mandatory. American Express will have lost a treasure in Sidney.

We were privileged to share Shabat dinner with him and his family at his home last Friday night. The love and respect they all shared is something I will never forget. I am honored to have met Sidney. He has made my life richer and more importantly has given me the gift of acceptance.

June 18, 2001 — Monday, 9:30 PM

Wrote a bit in shorthand today. Spent the rest of the day at the Marais, Bastille area, made an appointment at long last at a spa for Thursday. Quite an elegant and expensive one at that.

Tomorrow we plan on going to the Musee Marmaton and will do "Fodor's walk" of the area before. It was good to be on my own today and Peter feels the same. Found out that the synagogue at rue de la Roquette is Sephardic — wow!

June 19, 2001 — Tuesday, 10:00 PM

Visited the Marmaton which turned out to be my favorite art museum in Paris. All those Monets! It was wonderful, but apres, tried to do the Fodor walk and got lost (so what else is new.) We got to see one building, the Le Corbusier design for a home for a family named Roche. Built 1923 — 1925 and is ultra-modern even by today's standards.

When we got to our metro stop, we got out and had a cold drink and then made a wrong turn and walked forever. Collapsed on the couch and except for a quick trip downstairs to call my brother, and have been here ever since. And, of course, only CNN to keep me company. Missed yoga too. Not happy.

June 20, 2001 — Wednesday, 11:15 PM

Tomorrow is the first day of Summer and Paris greets it by having a fantastic and phenomenal day of free music throughout the city. The festival is called "La Fete de la Musique." To make room for the hordes of people and stages and performances, the buses stop running at 8:00 pm, but the metro goes all night. There are many choices — rock and pop, world, jazz, classical and dozens of performers in each category. Tomorrow at 12:30 pm, we are going to attempt to go to the Paris National Opera at my favorite building in Paris, the Palais Garnier. There will be arias, piano, chamber music, orchestras, percussion, and much more. And everything, all day and night is 100% free. In the evening will try to go to several places and stay out as late as we can. This event is my favorite day in Paris to date.

Peter is not feeling well: he has a cold. This morning I had my acrylic nails removed. This is a big deal. I have had acrylics for about twenty five! years. Just too difficult to find places to get this done. So now I have a regular manicure and my hands feel odd, lighter and the nails beaucoup short. We went to the Pompidou to see the Alfred Hitchcock retro. It was marvelous. I took notes for, maybe, articles for the Los Angeles County Museum of Art docent newsletter. I have been a docent there for many years. That is, if we ever get the computer working, a real drag. Had a bite around 4:00 pm at a small park near Chatelet. Had dinner at a veggie restaurant in the Marais. We walked there and back. The food was wonderful and trustworthy. Joseph, my brother, and sister-in-law Kate are now in Ireland. Would love to see them there. Peut- etre? Bon nuit.

June 23, 2001 — Saturday, 1:00 PM

Right now while Peter is out to the market, I must take a few moments to write about the utter and complete unhappiness I am feeling. My good spirits have plummeted. Big time. My beloved dog Lucy has been missing from our friend and keeper Efren. It seems she got out of his yard and chased a dog and then disappeared. She was seen intermittently in the neighborhood, but no one caught up with her. I am devastated as is Peter. I love her so much she is like my child to me. Efren is going all out in trying to get her back. He is offering $1,000 reward and I upped it to $2,000. I fear someone found her and since she is so loving and affectionate, the person is keeping her. She has dog tags, but no one called Efren. I have not given up hope but feel helpless and terrible. Paris has lost its light.

8:30 PM

Feeling a bit better due to distractions. Went to the gay and lesbian pride parade, which culminated at Republique, walkable from out apartment. Maybe, 20,000 people plus in the parade or viewing it. Quite a scene, but altogether manageable as everyone is so courteous. Tonight around 9:30 we are going to see a movie. Further distractions necessary. Got in touch with a few people e-mail today to ask their help in finding Lucy. This is just awful; Peter and I are grieving.

Le 24 Juin 2001 — Dimanche, 3:30 PM

I found out this morning it's is possible to grieve and have a good time in other ways at the same time, but then one hour later I cried my eyes out for a half-hour. My heart is broken, I can't believe I won't have my Lucy anymore.

We are in the Bois de Bologne, by the lake, having a picnic. It is cool here under a tree. Paris is hot today and we trudged along a path carrying food, etc. I want to see the Jardins, but we are too far away. This park is immense. My mother raved about her visits here. Peter is at last drawing and complaining that people passing by are moving! We had a fight this morning. I became angry at every little thing and, of course, my heart hurts and I wanted to lash out. I am angry that Peter is not sharing his grief with me; we feel and show it in different ways. He is terrified of negativity and bad feelings. I have to get my feelings out and there is no one here to do this with but he. So painful and frustrating. The movie last night was interesting but yet another downer; are there no American comedies in Paris? This is a time for me to write a story but I am too emotionally worn out. I won't even mention my body aches and pains. Psychosomatic? And where is there a toilette, when you need one?

June 25, 2001 — Monday, 7:30 PM

HOT HOT HOT — and no a/c anywhere. Peter is napping. I can't but wish I could. Tired and sad, sad and tired. We took a bus ride up, up, up to the northeast periphery of Paris to an area called Porte de la Villette. Discovered a huge and modern complex with an interesting looking science and industry museum. I'm talking gigantic and surrounded by water. Had lunch in the area and met our first nasty Parisian in the owner. It's so hard for us to eat out and so frustrating. Everything is meat or sauces. Managed to get a decent mushroom omelet, bussed part way back and walked downhill on a most charming street called rue Pyrenees, with smart little shops and trees lining both sides, very small town in feeling. I like this area a lot. We are going to the Wok Place for dinner. Maybe. The only relief I get from my heartache over losing Lucy is submerging into activity. Miss my Lucy so much, will she be mine again? I'm praying for this.

June 26, 2001 – Tuesday 5:00 p.m.

Losing track of the days. I'm sitting on the steps of l'Opera. I won't last long here because it is tres tres chaud ici and the sun is very strong. There aren't many of us here and there's usually a large crowd.

Went solo today. And there is a large sadness around everything I do. I cannot bear to look at dogs and I am surrounded by them. I so want my remaining days of Paris to be happy ones. Mais oui! This late morning I went to the Mode &Textile Musee. I bopped along rue de Rivoli as if it was Ventura Boulevard, intent on my destination. I stopped myself at one point. "Am I crazy?! I'm in Paris for goodness sake! PARIS!!" So I slowed down and smelled the coffee. The musee was so- so; far more interesting was an exhibit of 250 years of French advertising. Yes, they had posters as early at 1750. I am starting to broil and have to move to some shade. Am now in the shade with a bunch of gypsy women and kids who are running around begging and getting small change. Sad. I'll finish and move on. Had lunch at Galleries Lafayette after making a hair appointment through two interpreters for Monday. Don't think I'll keep it but look elsewhere. The nail deal is a fiasco;

they are awful without acrylics even after a manicure. Now to find a manicurist who understands.

Today is the first day of the big annual Galeries Lafayette sale. I spent 90 minutes looking. The shoe department is mammoth. I bet they have over 10,000 different shoes. And zillions of people. Way too stressful and tiring for me. And my feet hurt. My cute red shoes, that are so comfortable in Los Angeles are burning my feet. Glad, though, that I chose to dress nicely today — lifts my spirits.

Had a fun dinner at Wok and then walked to and hung around the Bastille. So much life there, it's amazing what having a beer seated at an outdoor cafe will do for one's mental state. We just returned from the cafe on Richard Lenoir that I like and took a little walk around the neighborhood. It's cooler outside than inside. Our apartment is on the 4'th floor and it's hotter than hell. The fan doesn't help much. It just moves around the hot air. I'm watching Tootsie in French. Last night I watched the Thomas Crown Affair in Italian. When it's a movie I've seen, I can do this and enjoy it.

I get a cafe du lait most every morning at a place called Cafe Anemones, which is right next to the metro and a few doors away from our apartment. After visiting for just a few days, I simply walk in and the young man behind the counter says bonjour and immediately makes my coffee. He doesn't need to ask me what I want. It's a nice feeling. I pay 9.50 francs standing at the bar and give him a one-franc tip. We chat in French, it's fun. We actually understand each other.

Tomorrow at 10:00 am I get my hair colored at a salon near here. I can only hope they do a good job. Bon nuit. Say a prayer for Lucy.

June 27, 2001 — Wednesday, 7:00 PM

An interesting day. Had my hair colored from 10:00 a.m to 1:00 p.m., very blond, about $90 bucks, dark roots and all.

10:30 PM

We should be asleep as we have to rise at 5:30 am. It's been an exciting night, not one but two phone calls and they were both for me, one from Gina who is now in Paris. Gina and I were in the same docent training class at LACMA. Los Angeles County Museum of Art. The other phone call was from my dear friend Beth. Great to hear from her! Xavier came by. I thought he would as we had made plans for dinner, but he never phoned, just showed up and we had already eaten so he visited. The French really do like to eat later in the evening.

This afternoon we went to an unusual museum called Musee Grevin. It was formerly a theatre and looks like a small version of Versailles. It was recommended by my friend Fabien from Les

Anemones. It has a fabulous ceiling, mirrors galore and full, and I mean full, of wax people who are or were famous, past and present and mostly French. I thought it was great. One very large room was a theatre. I'm sure it was a real theatre previously and was turned into this museum. And there were wax people seated and standing in the audience. Sorry I didn't have my camera. I am very impressed with this place, Peter less so. We walked a bit and then took the metro back. Never did get to do the laundry. Tomorrow is our bus trip very early in the morning. Hope I get to sleep fast.

June 28, 2001 — Thursday, 7:30 PM

We are in a Novotel Hotel in Caen. We awoke at 5:30 am and got on a Cityrama bus tour at 7:15. Our first stop was at 9:00 or so in Rouen. We hastily ate brioches, croissants, cafe and chocolat chaud and joined the tour leader in seeing the famous Cathedrale and then on to the square in town where Jeanne d'Arc was burned at the stake. There now is an ultra-modern church on the grounds. Onto a town called Bonfleur, a seaport and very picturesque. It was touristy, but in a cute way. We had lunch and walked and shopped. Back on the bus at 2:15 and headed for (quickly, too quickly) and through Trouville and Deauville which are summer resorts for the well to do French.

The most inspirational and truly awesome part of the day occurred at 4:00 p.m. when we visited the war monument in Caen. It is a very modern building, replete, with a complete history in items, pictures and films of French history of WWII up to the present. Peter being a history buff, loved it.

We viewed a 50-minute film in three theaters, moving from one to the other, about the war, and the liberation afterwards. I left quite moved and, in fact, cried a little. The last film showed Africa and the effects of war, all the starving and emaciated children. How stupid we all are and how inhumane to allow this.

Surely there is no need in this world for anyone to go hungry for even a day. The children are completely innocent and blameless. I feel ashamed of my complaining regarding my aches and pains.

At 8:00 pm we have dinner at this hotel. We have talked to no one all day and we've been with a full bus load of people for almost 12 hours. Strange. And somewhat alienating.

Le 29 Juin 2001 — Vendredi, 7:15 PM

We are on the bus returning to Paris after a very full day. We are to stop around 6:00 pm for a cafeteria type dinner at the Caen Memorial. We had a lovely dinner at the Novotel Hotel where we stayed last night and sat with five people from Taiwan who are visiting France for a conference on home science. They were all PhD's having studied in various schools in the U.S. Highly intelligent and very nice. One of the ladies gave me a back massage.

Today after 6:30 wakeup call and breakfast, we departed for the city of St. Malo and then on to Mont St. Michel. Spending a lot of time on the bus going to and from is trying. Mont St Michel is very impressive; an architectural wonder really, almost impossible to believe is was built in the 700's. Quite a climb to the top, but we did it. A tour of the incredible Abbaye and then down, down, down, to nothing but places to eat and souvenir shops. Peter is sleeping next to me. Lucky him.

I am in total awe of historic France, total awe. I will close my eyes now.

8:20 PM

Back on the bus since 7:00 p.m. and just passed Rouen. We see a sign that says "Paris 130 km" which translates to about 98 more miles. The driver is going tres rapide, but still is has to be at least two more hours to Paris. Too long. Our seats are very small as this is a different bus than our original. So, today, we will have been on a bus for about eight hours. have nothing to do on the bus, nothing to read, and nowhere to go. Feeling tired. Tomorrow is another full day. Wish I was interested in looking out the window, but it is mostly barren and dried up fields or clumps of green trees.

July 1, 2001 — Sunday, 3 PM

Dimanche, le premiere jour de Juillet 3:00 pm Fun writing in French. The first day of our last month here.

I am in bed resting, I have had a headache on and off for three days. It has been very hot and humid. I am a bit concerned because I do not normally get headaches, aspirin helps, but only a little. Tonight, we will have dinner in a restaurant with Sidney and Annette. They will pick us up at 7:30 pm.

Yesterday was another fabulous Parisian experience. Peter and I met Gina on Champs-Elysees which is now wall-to-wall tourists. We had lunch in the Marais at the restaurant across from the Parc des Vosges. The park was hosting Lavender Day and the entire park grass area was covered with pots full of lavender plants. Various venders were giving away lavender stalks and dabbing wrists with lavender oil. You could smell the scent of lavender for blocks from the parc. Gina filled us in on her life and activity at the museum back home. I feel so removed from all of this. We walked to the Bastille and I got a little dizzy, thousands of people on the streets, intense heat and high humidity. In the evening I surprised Peter with an evening at Au Lapin Agile in Montmartre. Gina and Xavier joined us. It was an incredible and for me a completely wonderful experience. Au Lapin Agile (agile rabbit) is an old-time cabaret. It is small and holds maybe 100 people. There are wooden tables with benches for seats. We were early and only 10

77

to 15 people were there. Then seven people sort of wandered in singing to the accompaniment of a piano. They sat together at a table in the center of the cabaret. Slowly, but surely, by 11 :00 p.m. the club was packed with Parisians singing along. The performers sang together and also had solos, all in French, songs we never heard of. Nevertheless, it was great! Never saw anything like this! Xavier was laughing a lot because, of course, he knew the words and some of it was simply storytelling put to music. We stayed about three hours. 130f included one drink served to us, a cerise liqueur. Xavier then took us for a car ride through Montmartre and we saw Le Sacre Coeur all lit up with hundreds of people in the area. He took us on the Champs-Elysees and at night it's an entirely different place, resplendent with nightclubs, cafes, lights and always hordes of people. The icing on the cake was a ride by the Seine, lit up by the buildings around it — gorgeous. To bed at 2:30 pm. Can you believe this? A completely glorious day.

July 2, 2001 — Monday, 10:30 PM

We had a lovely dinner with Sidney and Annette at a fish and wine restaurant near our apartment. Good food and pleasant company. Still had my headache, but less so after some wine. Went to bed, felt sleepy and thought I would fall asleep comfortably. Woke up at 3:15 p.m. terrified and very nervous. After several minutes of this, decided I couldn't handle this awful and fearful feeling. Took a xanax and fell asleep. Awoke at 7:30 a.m. Peter joined me and we stayed in bed until 11:00!

Left here at noon and went to Galleries Lafayette for serious shopping for gifts. With a short break for lunch, we were there until it closed at 7:00 pm. Managed to get petits cadeaux for the grand kids and shoes and sort of shirt/jacket for me on sale. VAT and 10% welcome card helped, but I am glad that's over — crowds everywhere — a mess and so hot. In Paris there are sales in the department stores just twice a year and one time is the month of July. The other is around Christmas.

Came home and relaxed and then at 8:30 pm or so, we took a bus to Belleville and were delighted by the beautiful park, which, after a zillion steps to the top, offers up a magnificent view of the city, all the way to the Left Bank. "My favorite place." Peter says.

Returned home to cleanup for the cleanup tomorrow. Meeting Gina at 1:00 pm at the Picasso Museum and lunch.

July 3, 2001 — Tuesday, 11:30 PM

Another day has flown by. Did e-mail this morning and then met Gina in the Marais for lunch. Picasso museum closed on Tuesdays so we went to the Jewish History Museum. First time for her, second for me. I loved it. Walked to the Bastille area, had a beer at a café and then took her to Tati. We both bought some cheap clothes; the store was mobbed. Gina came back to our apartment and the three of us went to dinner at the kosher Italian restaurant across the street. Quite good food. After a walk up, up, up rue Oberkampf to Belleville, Gina went home, as did we. Tomorrow, who knows? Opera Gamier for ballet at night, yay!

July 4, 2001 — Wednesday, 11:10 P.M.

There is an English movie on and I'll watch it a bit just to hear English. Just returned from the ballet at the Opera which was another evening of magic. The ballet, sort of a modern, A Mid-Summer Night's Dream was beautiful beyond belief. I saw it, but I didn't believe it. The choreography, costumes, sets, music and most of all the sensational dancers. I am completely in heaven.

The Opera house is the most magnificent building we have yet to see. I can't say that enough times. .Luckily, it rained tonight as the heat and humidity has been unbearable.

Did some errands this a.m. in the Leon Blum area. I like it around there with the cute shops, lots of trees, a pleasant little park and good patisseries. I like Monoprix a lot! Monoprix is a nicer version of a 5 and 10 cent store. Monoprix means one price if you haven't already guessed.

In the early p.m. we had our picnic snack on the Seine, watched the boats go by; it was so nice and temperate near the water. Days are disappearing. Just three more weeks in Paris.

July 5, 2001 — Thursday, 10:30 PM

Il pleut! Yeah! The rain is cooling off the city. We had dinner with Sigor, our next- door neighbor, who is returning to Amsterdam after a six-month stay in Paris. He is a writer and boy! does he ever let you know it. He is quite full of himself, but at the same time intensely bright and interesting. Went to the Chinese restaurant we discovered. I had more wine than usual.

We went to the Jardin des Plantes today which I thoroughly loved. Then a longish walk to the Arab Monde Institute which is in a great glass modern building, but we were disappointed in the scant free exhibit. Back to the room for a rest.

July 6, 2001 — Friday, 9:00 PM

Should clean, place is a mess, stuff everywhere, yada, yada. Peter is out to meet with Don, his childhood friend from days in Portland — bon chance! Has no clue where he is going.

I will meet them later in the Bastille area for a drink. If there was any semblance of a TV show, watchable in English, I stay put.

Today we bopped around. Started at the Forum at Les Halles, walked, bought shoes, walked, walked to Grand Boulevard, walked and walked some more. Years ago, Les Halles was THE place to go late at night (or very early in the morning) for onion soup. Had lunch at a cacher restaurant, a tuna fish sandwich and beer. A bit on the schlock side. Attempted to find the large synagogue on rue de la Victoire and failed. Took a metro to L'Etoile.

Walked. Took a metro to Sebastian area, full of fabrics stores and American restaurants, such as Hippo, Hard Rock Cafe, and KFC. Took notice of, on one of the very narrow streets, dozens of hookers! in broad daylight, unattractive, overweight, every few feet just standing around. It was upsetting. The men didn't look twice at them. Behind where they stood were narrow alleyways, I guess leading to the rooms. I happen to look up and saw a HUGE blue sign that said in up and down letters BEHAR, and on the door A. Behar! Behar is my maiden name. Peter and I were quite dumb founded. We discovered this to be an import export store and met four Behar's — very nice Turks from Istanbul. We will go back and take pictures. Home again and resting. Don just called. I will leave to meet them soon.

July 7, 2001 — Saturday night, 7:30 P.M.

Today we did very little. Woke up to rain thankfully. The city has cooled. We couldn't go to the Andre Citroen grounds due to the weather and the fact that we are both worn out. Peter slept until 11:00 and has laryngitis and a sore throat. We left the apartment at noon, with the intention of having an American breakfast (eggs) and then do our e-mail. Well, we were too late for breakfast, but we had a good lunch and spent about three hours on the internet. I was so glad to get mail from lots of people. After we decided to do a bit of food shopping and we went to the Leon Blum area; an area I particularly like for shopping.

Last night we met Don for a drink at the Bastille. I must say I had forgotten what he was like. A truly nice guy; I was impatient with his slowness, lack of excitement and almost complete lack of show of emotion. First time in Paris, first time in Europe! and quite blasé about it.

I had to wait 40 minutes for the two metros I take. The metros are slow and infrequent on the weekends. We are leaving Paris in less than 20 days. We leave soon and I can't bear it. I just love it here and feel so at home, at long last. I walk along the Boulevards as If I have always lived here. I should be reading about London but I am loathe to, not because I don't want to go there, but because it means leaving here. Peter is much more philosophical about this but I know he is attached to this place as well. Fabian my friend from Les Anenomes who has my café ready each morning, is gone on his two weeks' vacation in Spain, which means I probably won't see him again. I went to the cafe this morning for coffee and it was not fun at all. The people there are cordial but not overly friendly the way he was. We're having the most awful weather with lots of rain and cold, then the sun comes out for a while and then rain again. Actually, typical Paris weather. We sent all our cold weather clothes back to the States so we are left only with mostly summer things. I have so many emotions. I am sad and don't want to give this up. I still get excited each day when I leave the apartment and hit the street. I know my way around and enjoy this immensely. I know the shops and restaurants and marvel at how much we do each day. I have gotten attached to this little apartment. The only thing I miss is television in English. I just need a bit each night before going to bed.

My alone time in Paris is over. The Marjories start arriving in a few hours. I just love going around on my own and should have done more of this from the start.

Marjorie #1 is a very long-term friend I've known since I was in my 20's. She lives in New York City and early on we were neighbors in the same apartment house building.

Marjorie #2, who calls herself Margie, and I trained together at the docent program at LACMA. We discovered we lived near each other and became good friends. They are both the same age and met when Marjorie #1 visited me in Los Angeles.

We have slowed down a bit lately because we both are weary. But not much. There have been just few disappointments but perhaps my expectations were too high. I wanted to go to jazz clubs, go dancing, go to the Ritz Hotel, which I may still do when my friends arrive.

There is so much I could say about Paris. Where to begin and how not to be redundant. I need more time here. I am a bit apprehensive about moving on. It seems like a lot of work, the packing, flying, moving into a new place and most of all learning the new city.

Observaton. Icing on our gateau is the Belma's, Frenchmen and their bread, food in Paris, shopping in Paris, the courtesy of the young people, the education system, the Parisian view of the United States, all the slices of life that make up this trip, the people at the desk, Siger our neighbor, the patisserie lady, the yoga teacher, Fabien at Anenomes, the man who has beer at nine in the morning, my friends and their emails to me, the weather here, the optimism and much more.

July 8, 2001 — Sunday, 8:30

We just returned from dinner at the Italian restaurant across the street. Peter is writing in his journal. It is very quiet in here after the bustle of the streets.

We left here around 1:00 pm. I went out this morning to buy soy milk at the supermarche which closes at 1:00 pm on Sundays. Had a coffee at the Soleil. I don't like the vibes here and the coffee was 22f sitting outside which is 7f or a dollar more than my usual place charges. My place was closed today being Sunday, and beggars can't be choosers.

We traveled a lot today after saying it was going to be a restful day. We went to the movies at MK2 in the Bastille. Saw "Panic" with William Macy which was simply mediocre. I think all the bad or unreleased American movies come to Paris, but it was restful seated and I had some interest in the quirky film.

Afterward, we took a metro to the Nation area, a place we have not been, but seen as a metro stop. Save for the gigantic stone gates and pillars that led to the city in days of yore, this wasn't a particularly interesting area. Walked some to a metro that took us to Bellevue and the great park with its fantastic view of the city. We saw in a quite large lawn area, maybe 50 men singing, eating and we heard erratic music. No women in sight. Arabs or South Africans, Peter says.

Walked down to our street, had a good dinner and here we are. Haven't heard from Perry. Got an e-mail from him; he is in Paris July 7 — 11 and today is July 8 and no word. Perry is the teenage son of dear friends of ours who is touring Europe with a group. A really sweet guy and I look forward to seeing him.

9:00 PM Alors!

I'm not believing my eyes, a movie in English. It's black and white; "The Magnificent Ambersons," I think. I just drew the curtains and sitting up to watch and the phone rang twice. Business for Peter. We are once again unbelievably tired. Another full day. So, what else is new. Took a bus (was so proud of this) to Montparnasse and walked around and walked almost to the Louvre. Met Don there and had lunch in the Tuilleries. More walking. Apres, we shopped for gifts and Don came back to our apartment. Peter and I planned on doing a picnic, but were too tired so had leftovers here. Tomorrow we have lunch with Joan Grady and then a tour of Bercy Gardens. Hope to go to yoga in the evening, now that it's cooler.

July 10, 2001 — Tuesday, 7:00 PM

A day of some disappointments. Started out fine. We got grunge stuff done in the a.m. and met Joan at the Sarah Bernhardt Cafe at the Chatelet. Joan is Marjorie #1's friend from NYC and who now lives in Paris. It was sunny and warm. Left her for the metro to take us to Bercy. Metro not working and there was a huge crowd backed up on top the stairs. Left the metro with the idea of getting a taxi. No such luck and the rains began so we missed the tour in English of the Bercy Gardens. Disappointed.

Took the metro all the way to Belleville in hopes of seeing Edith Piaf Musee and after beaucoup walking found out it is only open by appointment! We wrote the phone number down, but will we go? Went to the internet place and found a message from Shelly who is Perry's mother, with Perry's number. His hotel was very near where we were so we walked there. He is out shopping at Galeries Lafayette. We plan on going back later. His group leaves at 10:00 pm for Lucerne by train, our little Perry!

July 11, 2001 — Wednesday, 10:15 PM

Our day apart. We went back to his hotel and surprised Perry. He is such a cutie. We were together about 45 minutes and then he left for Lucerne on a sleeping train.

Today was once again, full. Had a facial at the Intercontinental Hotel. I just love this stuff. Divine. Got lost. Went to Boulevard Etienne Marcel and discovered a whole new world of boutiques. Bought zero. Only a size two would look good in these clothes. Turned the corner and discovered a charming part of Les Halles, quite different from the very touristy and schlock other end. Lots of adorable restaurants. Sat down al fresco next to two gentlemen who were speaking English. I got involved in their conversations about films. "Bonjour madame." "Bonjour messieurs." They collaborated on a book about the director Max Ophuls ("Letter from an Unknown Woman.") I told them I saw this film. They were impressed, I think. My food was delicious. Chatted about half with them. Quite friendly, but I felt I was intrusive.

"Au revoir messieurs." "Au revoir Madame." I walked a bit and found myself in the wholesale clothing area, and got into the outlet of one of my favored stores, Gerard Darel. Almost bought a gorgeous jacket, but felt deceived regarding the price so at the last minute said no. The owner was quite angry. Tough. But. I may go back with Peter. Love the clothes there. Went to my haircut appointment two hours late, but they didn't seem to care. Pas de quoi.

My hair is tres court. Short — I'm talking SHORT. "I like it. You look very French!" This from Peter. Tonight, we went to the Mexican restaurant on Republique we have been eyeing for months, always seems so festive. We have been proved wrong — you CAN get a bad meal in Paris. We ate what seemed to be cactus. Have started packing for Federal Express, depressing. Don't want to leave here, decidedly.

Le 12 Juillet, 2001 — Thursday, 9:15 PM

Another day, another note book. Today was filled with many different emotions. It started out sadly because we packed a huge grey duffel with clothes and books and souvenirs to be picked up by Federal Express tomorrow. It feels like we are leaving here all too soon. I don't like this feeling. I made a few friendly acquaintances, know my way around, know where to go to get things at long last, feel more and more that this is our apartment, feel settled in and now we have to go. Just starting to feel at ease with not having to run around all over the place, getting a real sense of where I am.

A second feeling was excitement at the idea of having lunch at Le Train Bleu. In a word, it was fabulous; a magnificent room inside the train station, filled with frescoes, brocade, gold wooden statues, chandeliers, impeccable tables and service and food. Peter bought me a Le Train Bleu watch, which I love, for about $50.

Then, dejection because it was rainy and cold. We came home to change with the idea of braving the weather and perhaps going to Musee Picasso or back to the "Behar's."

At the apartment, Peter laid down and was OUT, wine and fatigue. I went to the internet place where I felt impatience, frustration and anger, because of my phone conversation with Efren, Lucy's caregiver. I would be doing so much more than he is with regard to finding Lucy. Peter is calling me to help with paperwork involving the Federal Express thing. A demain.

July 13, 2001 — Friday, 9:00 PM

I failed to mention that after a gorgeous Le Train Bleu lunch we had Mac Donald's, French fries and caramel sundaes for dinner. Today was a mish mosh. Started out early with Don and

Peter for the Picasso Museum. Walked from here to there. It was only 6/10ths of a mile and we didn't get lost. Spent a nice 90 minutes or so there. The grounds of the museum are almost as beautiful and interesting as the art within. Came back via metro at Bastille as the weather turned ugly, rain started. Don and I had lunch at Les Anemones where I said a sad farewell to Fabien (who reappeared after his vacation) and took pictures with him. He is such a nice boy. I shall miss my morning coffee with him. He asked me this morning, as usual, what are we going to do today? in English and I attempted to answer him in French. This was our daily routine. Don and I had a nice slow lunch while Peter took care of Fedex, which thankfully went well.

I like Don, but he is so slow in word and deed. I find this annoying and difficult. He seems to just go along, has no plans or ideas of his own. I hate this because, as with Peter, I have the role of leader, initiator, metro finder, etc. I love my husband so I do it for him, but doing this for Don just annoys me. After Don got settled, we went to St. Denis. Some hookers were out, but I think most of them were "working" or somewhere out of the rain. Went to the Behar building and took pictures with one of the Behar's with the large sign. Perhaps I will send him a copy.

We started walking towards Galeries Lafayette. Now the rainfall was heavy, so we took the metro.

I saw the Gerard Darel jacket I liked. It was 1646f at Galeries Lafayette and it was 1339f at the wholesaler. I am bummed out that I didn't get it and Peter might go out and get it for me at

Gerard Darel on the Left Bank. I don't have the nerve to go back alone.

We went to Gare St. Lazare, a very old and unattractive train station, especially compared to Gare de Lyon. I got the tickets to Vernon, the town of Giverny and Don got his Chunnel to London tickets.

A funny thing. It was teeming rain and I packed three pairs of comfortable winter shoes and sent them back to Los Angeles. I am left with sandals and mules. Also, packed away my raincoat! Who knew?

Tomorrow is the big Bastille parade and rain is predicted and I have no proper shoes. I went into a shoe store, near the apartment, on Republique and saw that the sign said open to 7:30. It is now 7:20. Anyway, they were having a small birthday celebration and closed early. I spotted a pair of white leather Keds. I BEGGED the proprietor to let me in to the store to buy them, telling her I didn't even need to try them on. She said no quite a lot, but finally broke down. Now I have a pair of Keds identical to the pair I have at home. I really didn't want white. No one wears white here. So 299f or $40 later I will be wearing these sneakers in the rain tomorrow and for sure they won't be white for long.

I am on the couch in my robe drinking tea, heating pad on my back, two aspirins in me, after taking what turned out to be a cold bath and semi watching a movie with Scott Bakula and Roseanne Arquette dubbed in Italian. Time to start reading about England, two weeks later than planned, oh well...

July 14, 2001 — Saturday, 9:00 pm

I just returned from the Champs-Elysees with Peter and Don. I left them to come home and rest while they will hang around and wait for fireworks which will be all over Paris tonight, especially around the Trocadero area.

What a day! Woke up 7:15 to a slight drizzle, left for the Champs Elysees to see the Bastille Day parade at 8:30 a.m. in a downpour. All the metros along the Champs Elysees were closed, so we had to exit at Madeleine and walked very circuitously — lots of police and blocked streets. There were a lot of bleachers and stands set up, but you had to have reservations. We couldn't even get near the Champs-Elysees, but stood on an adjoining street. Never was so wet in my entire life. Saw thousands of umbrellas and saw the parade clearly, but at a great distance. Most disappointing. Felt badly for Peter, who was looking forward to this day for months. After a few hours, the parade ended. We never did get to see the President, or Juan Carlos, or the review of the soldiers. Took the metro back to our area and had lunch at Leon's. We returned to the room with a short rest and then out to Parc Floral to see Dave Brubeck, something I had been looking forward to! Never got there. Too tired and too much rain. Headed out at 6:15 for a movie on the Champs Elysees and both theatres we were considering were sold out.

Took a walk down the Champs Elyees. Rain stopped, air warming up and we are suddenly stopped. Lots of police, traffic stopped, streets block off. Who came by with a police escort? Juan Carlos of Spain. I swear he looked right at me when I waved to him and he waved back. "Bonjour your majesty." Took a cab for 79f plus tip back, too tired to metro with three different trains. Happy I did. Now, laundry? Meeting Doris and Sheldon at 10:30 tomorrow morning. Today was a strange day filled with unfulfilled expectations. Doris and Sheldon are dear old friends. I've known Doris since kindergarten. Introduced her to the man she married, Sheldon. And now so many years later we meet up again in Paris. How great is that?!

July 15, 2001 — Sunday, 6:00 PM

I'm writing my journal earlier and earlier! Spent from 11 a.m. until 4 p.m. walking Paris with Doris and Sheldon. My oldest and dearest friends. I've known Doris since kindergarten! Great to see them and felt really bizarre, being with them in Paris! Childhood and lifelong friends, we don't see much of each other as we live on opposite coasts and now we rendezvous in Paris. Thrilling, actually! They are shoppers and wanted to go into many stores. Luckily, for me, most stores are closed on Sundays. I don't like shopping with others. We had fun, ate and drank and took pictures. An all too brief encounter. Left them at 4 p.m. at their bus and went to Montmartre for "tea dancing" at La Coupole, a very famous cabaret from the 1920s. Peter hated it there so we left after about 15 minutes. He said he felt depressed due to seeing "old" people in what he termed to be a dark and dingy place — said it made him feel old. It didn't bother me. I thought it was atmospheric. The DJ played rock and roll and then tangos and Peter didn't like this, nor the way people looked. I liked the ambiance. Made me feel French. We found the #96 bus in front of C& A and took it all the way back to Oberkampf. The weather was fabulous today — sunny and warm. We should have had this yesterday for the parade.

July 16, 2001 — Monday, 5:00 P.M

Beautiful weather. Had my café at Les Anemones, but not the same without Fabian. The two other men working there greet me and then say au revoir with nothing in between. I miss Fabian's daily greetings and interest. Went to the Gerard Darel discount house and the jacket was gone. Walked around Les Halles and discovered a most beautiful park area with a huge church St. Eustace, a beautiful park with an incredible large statue of a women's head and her hand holding up the head, in the plaza. Didn't have the camera, but Don took pictures. Took a few metros to get to Parc Monceau which is quite north of the Champs Elysees, a lovely area and perhaps the most beautiful park I've seen yet. The movie Gigi was filmed here. Don was the happiest I had seen him. Had a gallette and "coca" (rolled up crepe and coca cola) walked the park and then took a bus, another walk and a cab back. The boys are at the internet place. I had to return to fold the laundry that was strewn around the apartment to get dry. We are supposed to do Paris by night but I lost my incentive. I need mostly to rest. As I said before, I'd kill for an English language movie or show on TV.

July 17, 2001 — Tuesday, 6:30 PM

Awoke with a sore throat and tired body. Didn't do three out of the four things planned for today: no Richard Lenoir market for me. Peter went and bought fruit, vegetables and flowers. No Galeries Lafayette for the jacket and no airport to get Margie; Peter and Don will go to get her in a few minutes. Haven't heard from her which I find odd. I will go to bed and rest until they return.

Did go to the Bercy Parc in pouring rain and we were the only three on the tour. The very knowledgeable docent showed us the different phases of the garden, air, water, fire and the three gardens which includes the romantic gardens and a house that was a former winery, and is now a school for young people learning gardening. The two-hour tour, due to the strong wind and rain was shortened to about 75 minutes. We then went into Bercy Village, a cute new little area formerly a wine bottling area now restaurants, shops and movies.

We took the new metro #14 back. It is driverless, completely automated and goes a few stops just between Bercy and Madeleine. Now I'm resting and reflecting and feeling weary and sad. Also, I miss Fabien. Had cafe at the usual place, they are nice but not like Fabien.

July 18, 2001 — Wednesday, Midnight

Margie, Peter and Don returned to the apartment around 11:00 pm last night — not too bad. Good to see Margie. They brought her from the airport on the RER and when they got to Gare Du Nord, took the metro to the apartment. This made me a little angry. How do you do this to a 70 year old woman who has been traveling alone, from Los Angeles to Paris, for a whole day? We chatted awhile and then all went to sleep.

Today it poured buckets; this weather is impossible. Nevertheless, we set out at 11:30 a.m. for a walk in the Belleville and Pyrenees area. We went to the top of Belleville Park which is normally a spectacular spot. In this wind and rain, not enjoyable to me.

We kept our 1:00 p.m. rendez-vous to see the Edith Piaf Musee where, after secrets codes, two entrances, and a four story walk up, a gentleman let us into a small two room apartment. Edith is said to have lived there when she was young. I found it more interesting than I imagined. Strewn around the tiny apartment were books, pictures and tapes and her gold records. And in the background, we could hear Edith singing "La Vie en Rose," probably her most famous musical offering. I adored this outing. We had lunch at a brasserie in the Pyrenees area and it was bad, just an omelet but over cooked. Back to the apartment for a rest. Tonight, we went to dinner at Cote Du Seine on the Left Bank across a small street on the Seine. It was just so, so. Peter and I were there a few years ago and the food was great, this time not so much. Had a lively crowd, but on one side were loud and fat tourists from New Jersey. They did not fit into the ambiance. We spoke on the other side, to a charming twenty one year-old girl who was there alone. Gutsy, I think.

We pray for good weather tomorrow. We took a taxi both ways.

July 19, 2001 — Thursday, 10:30 PM

Gheez where do I start with today? We descended on Paris around 10:00 a.m. on metro. Marjorie No. 1 and I headed for the Left Bank. Spent a good deal of time walking around St. Germain de Pres, buying my Gerard Darel jacket, having a fight with Margie who is frugal and makes all kinds of wrongful assumptions because she doesn't listen. Met Peter at Galeries Lafayette for lunch. Took a metro to Les Halles and walked around dodging raindrops. Now the sun is out for a bit so we walked from Les Halles to the Left Bank, down boulevard St.

Michel all the way to the Luxembourg Gardens. Finally, walked back from St Michel to the No. 96 bus, I got off at Oberkampf and took the metro to the Internet place. Margie is a great walker. She settles today into the little apartment we rented for her in our building.

July 20, 2001 — Friday, 11:00 PM

Marjorie #2 arrived 7:30 p.m. today. Good to see her and in a few minutes, time felt like we had seen each other 10 minutes before. The two Marjories et moi trounced out at 10:00 am to petit dejeuner at my place but didn't like it much without Fabien. Headed for marche Richard Lenoir and we all bought some fruit. Margorie #2 bought me some lavender at the nearby florist. We then went out for the day with no rest. Visited Tuilleries, rue de Rivoli and then Musee Grevin. At 4:30 we had wine and cheese at a nearby outdoor café. This is something I wanted to do with Peter and never did, but with the two Marjories it was all very natural. Marjorie #2 fell asleep and then Peter, Marjorie #1 and I went out for dinner to a local restaurant and then — what else? More walking, goodnight to you all.

July 22, 2001 — Sunday, 1:00 PM

Yes! Dynamics changed when others come into your picture frame. Had breakfast at Les Anemones then went to the Left Bank to d'Orsay and it was closed. Peter and I went to the French Legion Museum — tres boring. On to the Pompidou for lunch al fresco. It is a glorious day weather wise, sunny and warm, made me happy. The two M's went to the Hitchcock exhibit and Peter and I took a walk. Back to the apartment for a short rest. Left the apartment at 9:00 p.m. and had a small dinner at a cafe near the Bastille. I had some wine and heard music and wanted so much to dance. Peter was being an old fuddy-duddy, so we came home. Monday, I shall have my birthday in Paris. We see Gina demain for a full day of Marmatton and Marais; is there anything I haven't seen in Paris? The two Marjories are very chatty with each other. Peter said I should be glad, takes the pressure off me, tee hee.

10:00 pm

And just where are the two Marjories? Out to dinner about an hour ago. It is finally hot and sunny and summer clothes are being worn.

We had breakfast downstairs today and took Marjorie #2 to St. Ambroise for mass. Marjorie #1, Peter and I, took a walk down rue de la Roquette, and went into both the Sephardic Temple and a very modern church. All of us went to the Marmatton where we met Gina. Peter and I wrote letters in the park and the five of us had crepes at a kiosk in the park. This is definitely one of my favored museums. So far.

Then, on to le Marais where Marjorie #1 and Gina went into the Picasso Museum. Marjorie #2 had tea at a local cafe and Peter and I walked and shopped. Next was a pit stop at Place des Vosges which was full of people on benches and on the lawn. We sat down for a while and then took a short walk-through rue des Rosiers to see all the Sunday Jewish action. Now, Peter and I are here alone, actually making lists regarding moving on Friday. I am depressed as hell about leaving. This has become home. This is a strange feeling, like losing a home twice within three months. See you tomorrow. Happy Birthday to me.

July 23, 2001 – Monday MY BIRTHDAY IN PARIS

12:10 p.m. technically in Paris, it is Tuesday July 24 and my birthday is over – but! I was born in New York and it's 6:10 pm there so it's still my birthday, so there.

Quite a day. Early breakfast with the two Marjories and Gina. Marjorie #1 and I spent the day together. Paid a short visit to place d'Opera, and then we went to Parc Monceau. Marjorie bought us a gourmet lunch and we had a picnic in the park complete with wine.

Apres le dejeuner we went to the Seine and ended up going up to the top of La Samaritaine, the large interesting department store smack in the middle of Paris. Great view and long lines for a drink at the outdoor bar. Back to the apartment and we had a glass or two of the Pommard wine I purchased on our Dijon trip. Peter was so sweet today, surprised me with lots of things, first a card with a beautiful message, then lovely red roses and finally a dinner party at, believe it or not, the Holiday Inn on Republique with the Marjories, Gina and Joan Grady. There was a cake with sparkles and Happy Birthday Allegreta written on it and champagne. The whole evening was just lovely.

July 24, 2001 – Tuesday, midnight

A superb day. Giverny. Gorgeous and wonderous. What words can express the beauty, naturalism, serenity and tranquility of a day here? Much has been written about this home and garden that Monet created. His art is everywhere; in the plants and brooks and bridges and decor in the house. We had a very special day at, for me, the most special place in France.

Then, more greatness. Xavier and Corinne brought me magnificent lilies. The tiny apartment is full of flowers, roses from Peter, roses from Joan, the little flower in pot from Marjorie #2 and lavender from Marjorie #1.

Splendiferous! Wish I could take all of them with me. We had a very enjoyable dinner with Xavier and Corinne at a restaurant near Leon Blum. So sad to say au revoir. Happily, saw much of them during this trip. Hopefully they will come to California. It's a good possibility. I like Xavier so much. He is such a fine person, so giving and caring. In later years he's become family.

Said goodbye to Marjorie #1. Looked forward to seeing the two Marjories for so long and now they are going or gone. We too shall be gone in a few days. I am so attached to Paris. Tomorrow is errand day. Marjorie #2 will go to Musee d'Orsay. I will meet up with her later. Today I am truly content. Sad about leaving here, sad about Lucy, but otherwise happy.

July 25, 2001 – Wednesday 11:40 pm

Another day gone by. The apartment looks like a cyclone hit, papers and flowers and birthday stuff everywhere. Loathe to give it up. The petals on the roses dropping from the intense heat; the white lilies putting up a brave and scentful front.

Just returned from Arc de Triomphe and had dinner on the Champs Elysees. Peter and Margie intended to walk up the 284 steps to the top only to find when we got there, it was about to close. I promised Peter we would go tomorrow. Today was an errand and shopping day. Margie and I walked about seven miles. It was very hot and when we came out of the restaurant apres le diner, we were delighted to see that it had rained while we were inside eating our dinner. The city had cooled off and the boulevard was enchanting, shiny and wet.

We took a taxi back along the Champs-Elysees and to the left of the Seine, the city all lit up for us. Evelyn, our friend from the internet place, is meeting us for petit dejeuner demain matin, between 9 and 10 a.m. She has been such a help to us and we saw a lot of her, being Peter's propensity for the internet. We promise to correspond via email. I shall start the packing process (ugh) and then laundry and then clean up. Maybe there will be a time for a final walk in our neighborhood park. One more entry in the book, tomorrow night. I can't believe that we are actually leaving.

July 27, 2001 – Thursday 12:15 pm

The last day in Paris. I am in the laundromat off of Oberkampf. There is about 40 minutes to go on each machine and then there is the dryer, the folding, the carting the stuff back to the apartment. I took a little stroll down Oberkampf and stopped at a shmata store that sells Eddie Bauer seersucker pants for 50f. Such a deal.

Observation. This neighborhood means a lot to me. I've gotten to know, if even slightly, some of the shop owners – the patisserie on the corner where Peter picks up his daily baguette, the shoe repair man who is Spanish from Chile and doesn't speak a word of English, the fromagerie which is tiny and also no one speaks English (a lot of gesturing goes on with regard to the size of the tranche of gruyere I buy for Peter), the supermarche whose hours are better than bankers, the tabac where I buy on Wednesday, my weekly Parisscope, Anemones my café and even the corner MacDonald's where I buy a coke and a sundae caramel, now and then.

And soon LONDON.

July 27, 2001 — Friday, 10:30 PM (11:30 PM Paris time)

Okay. So, I may be officially sick, coughing, sore throat. Merde.

Last night we had dinner at Renato's at Republique and the rains came. Big thunderstorm. Then we took a walk to the Temple Notre Dame de Nazareth, our last metro ride to Parmentier and a walk down St. Maur.

Packing was a nightmare, hotter than hell, too much stuff and purchase of another large duffel bag. Back to square one, we packed. Can't believe all this stuff. Such nonsense.

Had a decent seven hours sleep, awoke at 6:00 a.m. to continue the packing. Said goodbye to the staff and had a farewell cafe au lait at Les Anemones. Had a nice conversation with Patrick. I shall miss him and my café.

So, at 9:00 a.m. off to the airport, crowded and hot, people smoking everywhere. Six hours later we are in London, one hour in the air and 5 hours coming and going.

LONDON

We are staying at Nell Gwynne House. It is a very large apartment/hotel building right in the middle of Chelsea. I immediately like the neighborhood. Our one room is big with a separate small kitchen that includes washer and dryer. Had we known, I didn't need to spend two hours yesterday doing laundry. The fridge and freezer are in the main room.

English telly at last but not many stations and only one from the United States. Saw the very first Will and Grace. Peter made me hot tea; I'm grateful. Thank you, Peter, for taking care of me.

Earlier, took a bus ride to Piccadilly, which is disgusting and makes Broadway in New York look like the Champs Elysees. Or nearly. Lots of people, noise, Mac Donald's, Burger King, pizza parlors; everyone's young and seedy looking. Streets dirty, mayhem everywhere. Lots of theaters, which we will investigate tomorrow. London feels gigantic. Now there's a Street Wise London map in my purse after three months of Street Wise Paris. It's good to speak and hear English, but already I miss "Bonjour Madame." The sales people are not sociable, decidedly; maybe I'm just too tired and sick. Tomorrow, London will look better, for sure!

July 28, 2001 — Saturday, 2:30 PM London

Hmmm..Sick, headache, dreadful cough. Watching really bad TV in bed, but it is in English so it is a blessing. Peter is very tired, but went to the tourist office to line up a tour for tomorrow. And then he's venturing forth to get theatre tickets for the next twelve days we have here. The French party is over. Not a croissant in sight! I want to go out and see London, but Peter says I need to stay in bed. I don't think we'll be "discovering" here as in Paris. We will see the sights, go to theatre, then go through the dreaded process of packing, and must send more stuff home, essential. Then, the logistics of getting a car and getting a route. Perhaps three weeks here would have been a better plan. Now I must rest and read brochures.

July 29, 2001 — Sunday

If it's July, I must have a cold. It seems that I have been so sick in Europe, why is this? I now have a full-blown head cold with ugly green stuff coming from my chest in big coughs.

Today we did a lot and it is very hot . This flat has no air conditioning and I keep believing it will cool down. Very unusual for London at this time of the year. Or so we were told.

We started about 8:30 a.m. and took three BIGBUS tours and two walking tours, the first at 10:15 a.m. to see the changing of the guards at Buckingham Palace. Pretty awesome, I must say. The second was at 4:00 p.m. and was a tour through Soho of the clubs where rock bands of the 60's and 70's played including the Fab Four. I got to see PML, Paul McCartney, Ltd. Or McCartney publishing. Well, anyway, it was his nib's office building, and also the address 3 Saville Road that was Apple Music. Thrilling, actually. I am, like a lot of the world, such a big fan. Saw a lot of sights today, the usual London stuff, nice from the bus. Sat on top, probably not the best for my cold, but fun and interesting,

We see "Starlight Express" tomorrow night and plan on doing Harrods and the Tate Museum.

July 30, 2001 — Monday, 11 P.M.

Sweltering heat. A busy day in old London town. Started out too late. Peter went to a cyber place for a bit. Met him there and we walked through museum row to Kensington Gardens and Kensington Palace. I took a tour while Peter waited outside reading his paper. It was very interesting, not so much about Diana but about Victoria; she was born and lived there, as did other queens and kings. Saw the royal apartment and clothes and lots of other things to do with royalty. Kensington Gardens are just beautiful and just perfect. Had lunch at L'Orangery, a dining room set in a garden pavilion built for Queen Anne in 1704, right at the exit of Kensington Palace. We are feeling the cost difference between France and London. They charge a lot here for every little thing. I had a salad and they charged me extra for bread. Also, tips are not included and 10% is automatically added to the bill.

We walk more into Notting Hill, a vibrant, trendy area with casual cafes lining bohemian Portobello Road, famed for its busy market selling antiques and vintage fashioned. It was interesting at the start with antique shops and pashminas for L 7 (11 dollars), and then it turned into a Haight Ashbury kind of neighborhood. We took our first underground (subway) which turned out to be overground and a nightmare. We got stuck in a skuzzy area and no air conditioning and my head throbbing and nose running; couldn't wait to get out of there.

So far, I am not impressed with the Londoners, they are not as civil or nice as the Parisians. This is a tougher city — huge and loaded with people. Came back and rested and then took a bus, which I liked a lot better than the underground, to a theater near Victoria Station and saw our first London play, "Starlight Express." I found it tedious, too loud and frankly boring at the beginning but I did like the second act a lot better. We had excellent seats and the cast was roller skating all around us. Took a bus back and I want to sleep but Peter is on a business call. Living in one room is not easy. I 'm hoping to sweat this cold out with a lot of tea. Tomorrow, the Tate and some local sites plus a play in the evening.

July 31, 2001 — Tuesday, 10:30 PM

I have a lot of thoughts I need to jot down. I am writing with my new plastic aqua pen that says Tate on the clip on, very similar to my red Whitney pen. This cost 99 pence or about $1.45.

I am having a very weird experience, one I dreaded but felt it had to happen. I am in a foreign country and I am sick. Not horribly ill but I think it is either the flu or a very bad head cold. I've been ill a lot in Europe — I chalk this up to a change of air and food, being overly exhausted, emotions, etc. Anyway! I have coped and gone on. Now, we're in London with much to do and explore and I go through feelings of frustration because I want to do and see and sometimes I feel too sick to push through, and the other feeling is one of wanting to crawl and stay in bed.

Alas and alack, my ally the TV has failed me. We finally can watch television in English and the set broke somehow this morning. Most mysterious, it would be replaced, they say, tomorrow but I am not placing any bets.

I told Peter I was a little nervous about being sick here and he assured me he would always take care of me, but it is frustrating for him as well. I fervently hope I am well by the time we leave and the next week because just doing that takes an enormous amount of stamina and patience.

And where are we going anyway? Tomorrow we have to start on logistics — ugh! Today, we took a cab to the Tate, weather finally broke and it is cooler. Thankful for this. Spent a few nice hours there, including lunch. Really changing our eating habits. Swore off sweets for a week to start. Eating normal hours and eating small amounts. Walked down (or up?) the Thames to the Houses of the Parliament, Wesminister Abbey and purchased tickets for three events for next Monday. We start with a tour of the Houses of Parliament, followed by a tour of West Abbey, and then three royal apartments in Buckingham Palace. Took the bus back to Victoria station and collapsed for a few hours before going to the theatre.

I really like the buses here — they are fast, on time and we always get a seat plus a view — all this for a L. (pound). The play we saw was called Gondoliers and was a modern day adaptation of a Gilbert and Sullivan musical. Peter was disappointed because he expected Gilbert and Sullivan, I liked it. Last night the average age of the audience was probably no more than 20 and the average age of this audience was closer to 70!

Observation. About the Brits, I rather like the old guys. They have fabulous senses of humor, sometimes quite subtle and the older they are, the more their eyes twinkle. I have seen men easily in their 80's with full heads of white hair, clear blue eyes, on the thin side, running about. I find this adorable. And some have incredible stories, mostly wartime stuff . There is a lot I can say about the difference between the French and the Brits but comparison is odious. Right.

I decidedly do not like the Pakistanis here and there are a lot of them. They are very cold and unfriendly and disdainful of Americans. London is full of tourists and at least 50% are Americans if not more.

In the morning I forget that I am not in France and at least once a day so far I say "Bonjour madame s'il vous plait..." before I catch myself and realize they speak English like I do. Well, not exactly as I do, but close enough. I miss a lot of things about France and hearing French is one of them.

I promised Peter I would look for the miracle herbs that made me well last time. Now where would that be?

Tomorrow, maybe, we will visit the department stores Fortnum & Mason & Harrods, the British Museum and Bloomsbury. In that order. And if I feel up to it, a little pub crawl for Guinness stout and fish and chips. G'night mate!

August 1, 2001 — Wednesday, 11:30 PM
August! Already! How could that be?

Peter and I had a heart to heart today. I was feeling down about being ill and the little lonely and homesick and not all that enchanted with being in London, and at that point, no TV. We talked about a lot of aspects of our trip and ultimately came to the fact that we try to look at each new day with new eyes but if we don't not to chastise our souls. 180 days of just hanging out just is impossible and is terribly exhausting.

Today we walked to Harrods. This is the most amazing department store! So completely gorgeous and ritzy with the Egyptian influence everywhere. There are 23 places to eat from bagels to fine dining. I was enchanted by this truly spectacular store. We walked through Chelsea to Belgravia, a very upscale area with lovely mews, beautiful shops and very charming restaurants, to Victoria Station, where we took a bus to the British Museum. We had lunch there and stayed maybe another 90 minutes. Some stuff interesting, but generally not my cup of English tea. We took a cab back to rest before going to our third play "The Witches of Eastwick," a musical version of the stage play and movie which was great. Peter and I enjoyed it immensely. The leads, unknown to us, were fabulous and it was very entertaining. Tomorrow we go solo for half a day

I am a bit nervous about this but intend to go the Royal Academy of Art to see a Matisse and Ingres exhibit, and Fortnum & Mason. We have learned, in London you absolutely cannot do it all — it is too huge. I need a great night sleep. Bonne nuit chaps!

August 2, 2001 — Thursday, 9:45

Ran into a fellow docent from LACMA. What a rush to see a familiar face. I walked through Fortnum & Mason, the famous department store where I purchased tea, marmalade and a hair ornament. Had a pub lunch with Peter at a place called Zeeland's once owned by Sydney Chaplin and a landmark, near the internet place.

Although it wasn't a completely solo day, I enjoyed this alone time. I like hanging out in stores and museums without having to answer to anyone.

Having no plans beyond the next day is wonderful. Tomorrow we see "Mama Mia" — can't wait. Such a famous and well received show in the States. Plan on seeing Old Globe, Tate Modern and Saint Paul demain. Miss French.

August 3, 2001 — Friday, Midnight

Just got back from seeing "Mama Mia" — well, folks, good but definitely not great. Huge theater and at the end lots of dancing and singing in the aisles. Infectious for sure. But I don't know. Great expectations, maybe? Anyway, it was fun and hysterical actually how they put Abba's songs into the script. I love musicals but this one was wanting. I think I am the only one in the audience who thought so.

We left early and got a cafe du lait at the Chelsea Kitchen, this café could be my Les Anemones in London but I am not here long enough to cultivate this. Quel dommage.

We went by tube in a matter of minutes to the other side of the Thames to see the New Globe Theater. Peter took a walk while I took an interesting tour of the theater. We went practically next door to the Tate Modern, a fantastic large museum filled with modern art. I loved everything about this visit. We had lunch there — that's four lunches this week in museums. We walked on a bridge over the Thames to visit Saint Paul but they charged to go in and we just wanted a quick look see as we were quite tired by now. We easily found our number 22 bus right in front. It took about 45 minutes to get back. We are so impressed with the bus system here.

I phoned Jill and we arranged to visit her and stay at her home in Loxley for a day or two. Peter rented a car. We will make some plans this weekend. I am looking forward to company — another female to chat with! Jill is British. We met at a yoga retreat in Jamaica years ago and became fast friends.

August 4, 2001 — Saturday, 5 PM

The Queen mum's birthday — she is 101! Big doings at Clarence House where she lives near Buckingham Palace.

Last night at 12:30 pm, Eddie phoned. He put Carly, my granddaughter, on and she told me over and over again that she missed me very much — really touched my heart.

Today we took a walk up King's Road and strolled past many lovely shops and restaurants. It is a great area and I could live here very nicely. We went to a place called the Chelsea Bun for brunch; a wild place, very noisy, very happening. I had scotch pancakes — they came cold but I did not complain. We walked to the National Army Museum and then found the Chelsea Synagogue, which looked very upscale, but the door was locked so we couldn't see inside. We then took the number 22 bus to the end of the line, which turned out to be a boring area called Pulham, SW 15. We are in SW 3, so SW 15 is really west of the city.

Did some errands and back for a nap. Had a coughing fit this morning, which I thought would never stop. I am taking medicine and vitamins. What else can I do? Tonight, we see "R Shakespeare" and oh! got an email from our dear friend Mitchel. He very matter of factly mentioned that he broke up with Leilani. Peter and I turned to each other and said WOW. I can now say, many years later, they reunited and married. Had to put that in. Happy ending. I am facing a scary thing — will attempt to do laundry in a washer-dryer before we leave. Yikes!

August 5, 2001 — Sunday, 10:30 PM

Sick, threw up cough medicine at the Safeway, stayed in, feeling sorry for myself. Play last night was nothing special. Thus far we are somewhat disappointed in our theatrical viewings, pray to feel better, watching movies all day on TV, tomorrow better, amen.

August 6, 2001 — Monday, 6 PM

The sun is out — finally. My handwriting is as erratic as this day. Got out early, 8:30 a.m. On our way to visiting Houses of Parliament in the morning and Queen's apartment early afternoon. Got on the bus feeling lousy and found that somehow the tickets for both events went missing.

A real mystery, because I put them in Peter's backpack right before we left. We got to the Houses of Parliament and luckily, they let us in after a bit of a wait in the rain. It was a very interesting tour seeing how English government works and the halls, waiting rooms, and especially the House of Lords were spectacular. After, we went to Buckingham Palace to see about the afternoon tickets but they wouldn't do anything for us. I was very disappointed, especially since I felt so sick and still attempted to go. We came back and rested a bit, and then I said, "Let's go to Abbey Road!" We figured out the tubes and it was about a 45 minutes trip each way, two changes and a not so short walk, but for me well worth it. I got chills walking across Abbey Road, which was one of the Beatles' album covers. We came back and had dinner early at an Italian restaurant. I have no appetite but feel I should eat. After a hot bath, I will dress for our sixth play, "Blood Brothers" and pray the sunshine lasts.

August 7, 2001 — Tuesday, 6:30 PM

Well, I did it. I went to a doctor today. I just felt awful and a long and short of it is I have a viral infection. Not such a big surprise. So, L88 ($ 135) later he gave me a prescription for a bunch of stuff and I even got one for an antibiotic but I am not to take it unless I get worse. I shuddered at the thought. Spent the whole day in bed, that 3 days out of a 14-day trip. The weather is awful — I just hate it — can't run around — it is cold and windy and rainy — in August. There will be a lot of things I want to do here that will remain undone. I inhale, took a cold medicine, gargled and took antihistamine. The rest is rest! Bummer.

I hope to be a lot better by tomorrow as we go to Claridges for tea and our final theater outing.

So much stuff to do to get out of here and Peter is at the internet place again; he has communication problems, always problems.

August 8, 2001 — Wednesday, 1:30 PM

Peter is out at a business meeting. I am in bed feeling shitty and also as depressed as I have ever been on this trip. It is said that writing is a good catharsis, so I am writing.

Feel a bit nauseated from all this medicine. We changed Claridges to tomorrow. So much to do to get ready to get out of here.

This weather is the pits. I don't know why anyone lives here. Haven't really seen the sun since we left Paris. I am so spoiled with California weather. This town requires a ton of energy and my whole system is a mess. I am having a bad day. I long for the comfort of our home I no longer have and my Lucy. My heart will not mend over her loss. I should get up and move around and do a few things to get ready but I have no desire or strength, Paris was so wonderful and this is so NOT. Yet, I have learned a little bit about London and I am interested in knowing more. I think Zen.

The play was good, not scary and we met a man who teaches at Dowling College on Long Island where my brother teaches. This man says he knows my brother slightly.

August 9, 2001 — Thursday, 7 PM

Our last night in London and Peter is at the Internet place for the second time today and I am in our room packing.

Another terrible day weather wise. Rain and more rain. I went to do email earlier and I have 197 messages. Had high tea at Claridges at 3 pm, there was a string quartet and the whole experience was very chic. The ambiance was wonderful. Not a lot of people in this magnificent old hotel until about 4 p.m. We had tea and little sandwiches and scones and pastries. We stayed about two hours, I loved it. I felt elegant. We took cabs both ways. Can't even take a nice walk in this weather and having this cold. I would love to walk in the gardens and parks but how can I in this down pour? We are bummed out. London did not live up to my expectations. And so, goodbye London.

August 10, 2001 — Friday, 10 PM

Where to begin. Awoke early, a.m. or so and stayed in bed until 8:30, dreading what lay ahead. Got more packed and we decided to send more stuff back home. I am not feeling much better and I called the doctor who was very sympathetic but couldn't do anything except tell me to REST.

Peter went to Federal Express and I tool a little walk on Kings Road. Finally, some sun and what a difference good weather makes.

Coffee at Pret a Manger and looked in the shops. London is so nice in good weather. Then, we got in the rental car and it is so weird, I sit up front on the left and Peter is on the right. Then we took off. My stomach will never be the same. It was very uncomfortable— a double whammy — driving on the left was hard enough but not knowing where we are going and getting lost several times does not make for a pleasant trip.

THE ENGLISH COUNTRYSIDE

Peter's wheels kept hitting the left side of the road and then after we got lost trying to find Oxford, we kept circling trying to find a place to stay. We found, after many people gave us bad directions (and why is that I wonder?) an adorable B&B called the Pickwick House. It is really pretty and spacious with a lovely view of a backyard with pond, trees, patio, etc. The room sleeps three so we have an extra bed to dump stuff on and do we have stuff! We left our large duffel, jackets and a few small bags in the trunk. Hope no one breaks in. Poor Peter is so stressed out from the driving. Tomorrow we bus into Oxford — thankfully not driving. It will be a full day and I am coughing again. G'NIT' LUV

August 11, 2001 — Saturday, 11 10 P M

Another day full of activities, we slept okay but awoke at 6 a.m. Went to breakfast at the B&B and it was adorable. We ate in a sweet room with about 12 small tables overlooking a garden. There was a sidebar full all of kinds of cereals, fruits, three kinds of juice, coffee and tea. A nice lady takes our order for eggs and we could have meat, beans, hash browns, bread, stewed tomatoes and mushrooms as well.

The room we have is charming and has everything including an over the head TV, radio, phone and fresh towels and sheets each day. Very English country in feeling. Which is where we are.

We went into the center of Oxford by bus and took a city tour. We sat on top to see well and it was cold, windy, and a little rainy, Weather sucks -- I am wearing a tee-shirt, sweats and a blazer. In August!

Had scones and tea in a restaurant, inside the university. It looks like a church as well. Took a walking tour led by an amazing 71-year-old lady who turned out to be Jewish and who lived in Poland through the war openly making vodka in the country side! She showed us all the colleges and we got to go into two, including Christ Church, the grandest. There are 36 colleges in all and we got to see about ten. So much history and so many really old and grand buildings. A great and interesting tour. Afterwards, we went to the oldes pub in Oxford, dates back to 1242! It's called the Bear where we "had a pint." The pub is small with a very low ceiling and there are thousands of men's ties from golf clubs all over the ceilings and walls. It would take a day to look at them all.

Came back, took a short rest and then went down the road apiece and had dinner at a very lovely Greek restaurant. Tomorrow, we may visit Blenheim Palace where Churchill was born and then on to Jill's. I pray we don't get lost and that the driving is better for Peter.

August 12, 2001 — Sunday, 10 PM

Well! Guess where we are? In Loxley. Where is this exactly? It's near Stratford on Avon. We left the B&B and headed for Blenheim Palace, which we reached with ease. Weather ghastly. Unspeakable. Spent four hours touring the palace and walking the grounds — there are 2100 acres in all! Quite a joint. Churchill was born here. It is truly a stunning palace and now the tenth Duke of Marlboro and family live in private quarters here. The gardens have a cascade, a huge rose garden and lots of green everywhere. We left and got to Stratford around 4 p.m. but it was full of people so we headed out to Loxley and after a few mishaps, here we are, in the middle of the country in a genuine Victorian cottage. We had a great dinner with Jill, her husband Mick and two of their friends. Really good seeing Jill and meeting Mick, who greeted us warmly. Tomorrow we get the cook's tour.

August 13, 2001 — Monday, 11 PM

A great day. Had a leisurely morning and walked around Jill and Mick's property, which has three separate gardens areas, one with wild flowers, another with herbs and vegetables. Jill makes her own currant jelly. We left around noon for a tour through the Cotswolds — small English towns, cobblestones, bleached yellows tones, little pubs and a very old Agoura — since 1600 — in the center of the one town we walked. After lunch, we went to Hindecott Gardens, which is virtually indescribable but I will try; gigantic lawns and fields of flowers and trees, very spacious and glorious greenery everywhere.

Approached an area called the "HAHA" which was an enormous field full of grazing sheep as far as the eye see. There is a light stonewall at the approach, followed by a ditch, so you can sit on the wall but cannot go over it onto the field. And the sheep cannot get out.

On this property is an area called the Maize Maze that has to be seen to be believed. Six and half acres of a maze of corn and sunflowers taller than us we are. When you enter the maze, you are given a colored flag which is on a long stick and you carry it over your head so others can keep track of you. In the middle of the maze are two bridges and from the top of the bridge you can see the top of the maze and everyone's flag. It took Jill and I 40 minutes to get out and Mick and Peter only about 25 minutes and we needed their help. We were all thoroughly exhausted as we did this excursion after walking to the towns and walking through the gardens. We decided to eat in and Jill, from nothing, made a superb meal of leek soup, pasta and I made a salad. It was nice cooking in an actual kitchen. Mick and Jill are just lovely people, so charming and gracious. Tomorrow Jill and I will have lunch and shop in Stratford and meet the men at a house Mick and Jill own. I am more relaxed here than I have been in while and I think that the fact that the sun was out today is a big factor. Also, this has been the first few days where we are taken care of and don't drive or have to make any plans or decisions. And we are in a house. All of this comes as quite a relief, much to my surprise.

August 14, 2001 – Tuesday 11:30 pm

Lots of fun today. Left around 11 a.m. and went into Stratford with Jill. We had a heart-to-heart talk, like we did when we were together in Jamaica. We walked around this beautiful town, Shakespeare stuff everywhere – where he was born, Anne Hathaway's cottage, Mary Arden's home (Shakespeare's mum) the theater and more, and of course, the river Avon. We had lunch at The Vintner's and I bought a pair of stretchy pants at Mark & Spencer for L.25.

Later I met up with Peter and took a tourist bus ride for an hour around Stratford atop the bus. The sun is shining and it is warm. Yay!

Returned and had dinner here with Mick and Jill and their son Jem and two of their friends. In fact, the two friends are still here but I excused myself to go to bed. They are drinking what seems to me to be a bit much more wine and now, after dinner drinks. I was getting bored with the conversation. Jill gets more exuberant as the night proceeds. They are very good souls and most giving and gracious towards us. This is a very comfortable place to be and I shall miss the bed, and especially the gorgeous unkempt garden. Tomorrow we head for a place called Owl.

August 15, 2001 – Thursday

Yesterday, Wednesday was one of those days that are partially good and partially a nightmare. Started out nicely enough. We hung out at Jill and Mick's until about 1 pm and even got to use Mick's internet, and the sun was out. Did laundry and packed and then off to Cheltenham, about an hour's drive south. Got there and got lost; so many one-way streets, but not a big deal. Had a late lunch al fresco at the Montpelier wine bar and had my first Caesar salad since leaving the US. Took a walk around town, a really charming but not small city with a magnificent large open garden full of very colorful flowers. Visited the Queen Hotel, old and splendid and Roman looking. Very upscale shops. Headed for who knows where and Peter was tired so we decided around 5 pm to look for a B&B. Three and half hours and many stops later, we found the Stonehouse Court Hotel where we are now, staying both Wednesday and Thursday. We even tried getting into a Travelodge and they were completely booked. This hotel is very posh and has lot of stone. It has a very grand looking lobby, restaurant, a gym and gorgeous gardens facing water. The English do love their gardens. 90 pounds for Wednesday night and 70 pounds for Thursday night. We decided to stay the extra night as this was a glorious place to be and Peter needed a respite from driving. The place we want to visit, Gloucester, is only 30 minutes' drive North.

A word or two about the driving – MOST STRESSFUL for both of us. And not knowing where we are going while driving on the left side of the road is uncomfortable and daunting. Peter doesn't get to see anything of the countryside because he is so intense about his driving. I shudder when he gets too close to the left curb, the side I am on. The hubcaps are taking a beating.

Today we took a wonderful walk in the country, which is right behind our hotel. There is a stream and a few fields of cows. Mad cow disease warnings are posted. We met a few men and boys fishing the stream and we also chatted with an elderly couple on bikes. On our way back I fed some ducks bread from a bridge and we met a man named Mike who magically had the keys to a wonderful old church and cemetery nearby. It is about 500 years old. And grave stones! 100 years old.

Gloucester was fair. We took a boring 45-minute cruise and we were both disappointed in the Dock, which is highly advertised as an interesting and famous place to see. We then walked into town center and were not impressed, kind of a lower-class place with ugly or vacant storefronts. And not at all interesting.

Upon our return we stopped for dinner at Woolman's, a pub and restaurant in the town of Stonehouse. We had beer and fish and chips. We met a very interesting man, also named Peter, who told us quite a lot about the area and offered suggestions of places to go. I am happy now to lay in bed, watch TV, maybe take a bath and go to sleep early. The room is large, luxurious and warm.

August 18, 2001 – Saturday, 9AM

Once more I left my book and Tate pen in the car yesterday and Peter fetched the book for me, sans pen. I am writing with my Whitney pen now. Yesterday, like other days we drive, was both great and a nightmare. We started out taking a lovely walk and taking pictures of the back of the hotel. Had a wonderful English breakfast in the hotel's beautiful and quiet dining room. Left around 11 a.m. for Cowslip – a magnificent spot – arguably the most scenically beautiful spot in England. The grounds house a manor with acres of gardens and old Roman baths far into the countryside. The manor, alas, didn't open until 2 pm and we were there at noon. We sneaked into the gardens and saw a small part of the manor and the ancient hall turned into a restaurant. I desperately wanted to stay in one of the nine cottages they rent but Peter didn't, so we went on to Bath. Of course, we had to stop many times for directions. Driving here is the pits. No one gives clear directions and so many streets in the towns and cities are one way, or, as they say here "one way system." We finally got to Bath, parked and got a place to stay, the Francis Hotel in Queens Square, really nice, very old, originally built in the 1700s. Peter suggested we go to a movie and we went to an actual theater and saw "Planet of the Apes." It is a movie, right? Sleep and tomorrow touring in the rain.

6:00 pm Just finished having our tea with biscuits in our room. Every place we have stayed thus far has provided us with an electric teapot, cups and saucers to match, choice of tea, coffee, milk powder, sugar. And biscuits as well.

Next day, I had a wonderful time at Continental breakfast. At 9:30 we went to the Pump Room restaurant inside the Roman bath building. It is tres elegant, a large room with chandeliers, tables with white linen tablecloths and napkins. I was the first to arrive and had Continental breakfast which consisted of coffee, croissant and orange juice. The bill came to L4.95 and a tip of 80 pence. The icing on the cake and the reason I was there was to experience the three-piece musical group, cello, piano, and violin. They started playing at 10:00 in the morning! Imagine, breakfast with live classical music. By the time I left to meet Peter at 10:30

the room was completely filled and had a waiting queue. We took a three-hour walking tour of historical Bath that was too long. It was interesting, but the guide, a very proper Brit lady told us way more than we needed to know about the history of Bath. In town later we had fish and chips as there was a thirty-minute wait at the veggie restaurant where we wanted to eat. We split up and I walked the great shops, got some herbal stuff for my infected finger and mustard seed bath powders, did an hour of internet and finally, with remarkable ease got to erase 200 junk mail messages.

August 19, 2001 – Sunday 5:30 pm

Last night we had a quick bite in a café in this historical hotel and then went to something called "Bizarre Bath", a one-man guide through Bath with absolutely no historical value; just for laughs. It was quite funny. The Brits have the best sense of humor. I have noticed that wherever we go lately we seem to settle into a mini routine, like yesterday, we just had our tea in our room, having to split up around 3 pm today. We arouse late and stayed in bed until 10 a.m. We had a good breakfast at a place called California Kitchen. We then took a one hour boat ride down the Avon which was very pleasant. No rain at this point. We then took a long walk on a path next to the river, circling the city and walk back to the City Center, which is where we separated. I went to the Costume Museum and enjoyed the exhibit a lot, especially a special show on fashions of the 1950s. We are resting now and plan on going to a Chinese restaurant for dinner. Then, the inevitable packing up.

10:00 pm

Had dinner at Chinese restaurant and was disappointed that it was a "family" restaurant in that I wanted something with music and nightlife. I took particular care with clothes and makeup. I drank wine and got spacey. And wanted to dance and carry on. But no. Tomorrow we go to Stonehenge.

August 21, 2001 – Tuesday 7:30 pm

I skipped yesterday because once again I left my notebook in our car. And guess what? I made a faux pas. I was positive we were to leave for Rome on Friday, when in fact we don't leave until next Tuesday, August 28th. It seems that in my mind we had two weeks in London and two weeks in the country, which adds up to 28 days. We were at this point all packed up. We found Stonehenge pretty easily. After stopping on the way at a town called Amesbury, we had the worst breakfasts of our life at a place called Friar Tuck. Stonehenge is as amazing and awesome as I thought – how can one describe this? Parts of the Agoura are still standing and artfully preserved. A very spiritual place. Humbled, shocked, awed. This place is 4000 years old! And people lived and shopped here. I could actually visualize them, winding through the streets, going into the shops. We drove a bit and landed in a town close to old Salisbury. Turned out to be very charming, the inevitable river running to a park and to a town with shops, restaurants and a magnificent cathedral. Maybe the grandest one we seen yet. We got a room at a B&B about 15 minutes' walk from town center. It is really nice and large with a canopy four poster bed, side tables covered with lace cloths, flowered wallpaper, white love seats, pink tie back drapes, large bathroom and of course! – a tea service and biscuits. There is also a sitting room and a very nice dining room in a glass walled garden area. We are happy with this place. After a quick bite we went on a 90-minute city walking tour and as we were the only ones on the tour, the guide tailored it to us. Cab back!

Today, Tuesday we had a lovey breakfast and then walked, via the river path into town. We visited a large outdoor market, which is held just on Tuesdays and Saturdays. We then toured the cathedral and saw one of the only four remaining copies of the original Magna Carta. Chilling. We had lunch in a church refectory area. I left Peter to tour a pre-Victorian house in an adjoining area called The Close, 13 homes originally built for important heads of the cathedral. We were going to rest and then go out again for dinner but as we were tired, we picked up sandwiches and cookies and pudding and I made tea and we ate in the room. There is a piano downstairs and I am tempted. Laying in this bed, writing in this book and listening to an English soap opera is delicious.

LA SACRESTIA
ISTORANTE
ARIA CONDIZIONATA
Caffé Ristorante
La
Sacrestia
FORNO A LEGNA

BRIGHTON

August 23, 2001 – Wednesday 10 pm

Peter's birthday was yesterday. Every day is special on this trip, so we didn't do anything special to celebrate. We are now comfortably ensconced at the Thistles Hotel on the beach at Brighton. It was fairly simple to get here, only one wrong turn in a day. We are paying a lot for this place, L96 per day which includes parking. We didn't know it but Monday is a bank holiday and all the cutesy el cheapo beach places are booked for the long weekend. We didn't search for but found this place, and it is logistically where we want to be. We have a really nice large room. After resting a bit we had a good lunch at an outdoor restaurant called Boardwalk. I had vegetarian bangers and mash. Peter asks, "what are you eating." I told him I have no idea. We walked on to the edge of the water and discovered that the beach had no sand, only very large pebbles. We went on to the very famous Brighton Pier which is miles long and wide and full of various amusements including gambling, rides, video stuff, restaurant and food stands. So now I've seen it and don't have to go back. I mean, we have the Venice Pier, right? Venice, California that is. Tomorrow I plan on doing some spa stuff, maybe at the Grand Hotel, which is aptly named, and is the best hotel in Brighton. Big bucks.

August 23, 2001- Thursday 9 pm

Relaxing in bed, watching an English soap opera on a decent size TV screen – maybe 21 inches? Biggest one yet on this trip. Took an early walk but no sun today. Went to Boots for meds and then a horrible breakfast. Walked to town and found a veggie restaurant that has live music at night and so we had dinner there and I enjoyed it a lot. If a restaurant has music I don't much care about the food. I have a massage at 4:30 in the room preceded by a sauna in the gym in the hotel. Took a short walk apres le diner. I have a 9 am facial scheduled for tomorrow and then we are going on a tour of the Pavilion followed in the evening by synagogue and dancing!

August 24, 2001 – Friday 9 pm

I have been in the hotel room since 3 pm. I will get dressed soon and we are going dancing. Yes! After talking about it for months! Today I had a wonderful facial at a salon above a Body Shop. We have lots of Body Shops in the states but no salons. Peter met me after and we went to see the Pavillion, the Chinese Fantasy Castle of George IV, then Victoria, who sold it to Brighton in 1850 because the area became too crowded for her! I loved it; gloriously Chinese. And incredibly beautiful. I bought yet another little decorative box from the gift shop. I love it. We had a so-so lunch at an outdoor café. Peter says "It is true that the food in England is as bad as the food in France is good." I agree.

We walked to The Lanes north and south and then the beach area which was quite foggy. The crowds are coming in to Brighton. We came back to rest at 3 pm and Peter went out to get sandwiches for dinner. Too difficult to go to synagogue. We are disappointed.

August 25, 2001 – Saturday 8:30 pm

Our attempt to go dancing last night was a DISASTER. The evening was a floppero and a huge disappointment. Dancing didn't start until midnight. After resting and preparing most of the day, we got to the club at 11pm. Nothing was happening. We left at midnight as we were tired of just waiting around and just as we were leaving, very young people were lining up to come into the club. I really wanted to dance but I knew this was not going to be our venue. Best not to have expectations.

Today, it is all fun and games. Had a lovely breakfast at the hotel overlooking the beach. It is a completely sunny and warm day at last. Food sucks big time. The Brits even screwed up the croissant, stewed fruits and coffee. Went to have my roots touched up at Tony & Guy. They were so nice and gracious to me. My hair is very dark at the roots, and the blond sections need work but I was putting it off. Afterward, we took a bus ride in and out of town which was only mildly interesting. Then a bit of rest before dinner at Terre a Terre, a gourmet vegetarian restaurant. Expensive but worth it. We took a walk along the water. It is very happening tonight as thousands of people are in Brighton for the weekend. We are planning on a swim in the pool tomorrow and then – yuck –laundry.

August 26, 2001 -- Sunday 3 P.M

The Maltese Falcon just started on TMC. The oldest movies are shown here; last night was "Soylent Green." We had an interesting morning – very. Went swimming in the pool and took a sauna at 9 a.m. then on to a local spot for breakfast where the orange juice is L.2.95 which is about $4.50 so we passed it up for coffee and scones and Peter had eggs. Took a long walk on the boardwalk west and discovered that the boardwalk widened to become a very wide and long promenade, as the beach narrowed. Suddenly it started to rain and then pour. We found shelter at an enclosed bench; there are several on the promenade facing the sea. A very interesting Brit from Hove, a little town that runs into Brighton, started talking to us and we found out the Brits decidedly don't like the French. He told us fascinating stories about the Queen, Queen Mum, Charlie and all the other Royals. Also got into American politics. The Brits think very little of George W, that's for sure. We walked back on the street side and saw the most beautiful yellow painted townhouses and parks and the Metropole and Grand Hotels. Did a bit of internet and back to the room for a rest. The rain let up. Lots of thunder and lightning for about 30 minutes and then the clouds moved away. Amazing. We did laundry. It is easy when you can actually read the instructions on the washing machine. After a while, we took a drive to see Hove, which is an upscale richer Brighton. We returned to the room and then went down to the bar here in the hotel; its name is WWW Water. I had a martini. First one in Europe and it was dreadful. Oh well. Tomorrow we drive to a hotel near the airport and Tuesday we go to Rome. Yes!

August 27, 2001 – Monday, 8:30 pm

It looks like I will be finished with this note book just as our stay in England is over. We are at a hotel by Heathrow Airport. It is cheap. We had a swim and a sauna before leaving our lovely hotel in Brighton. A beautiful day – sunny and warm. Had breakfast in The Lanes and took an hour stroll there followed by a short walk on the beach and then we drove here. Brighton was nice, restful, beachy and lively. And a little luxurious as well. I shall miss it. I could live there. I even drove a little. Peter was terrified! But I think I did okay. No cars around. Tomorrow Roma!

Peter is returning the car to the airport. I packed up as much as I can without his help. It is a challenge trying to get everything into these suitcases!

Observation. Looking back at this month, I see that England was so difficult and yet so great for us. London was exciting and hectic – so much to see and do – so much history. There was the never-ending saga of the Royals. Chelsea, where we stayed for two weeks, is so interesting and pretty, the theater while not great still a very worthwhile experience. I think Peter was more disappointed than I, he read about London Theater and the West End and I think he thought it was going to be fine and fabulous. The countryside was truly enchanting and a delight – all those meadows with sheep. The gardens – the Cotswolds and all the charming towns. All that stonework. Our wonderful stay with friends at Loxley. Bath – a town I loved. Salisbury, so charming with The Close. And Brighton – great in the sun when there was sun. I liked the ease of the beach city and the ability to walk everywhere. The downsides – the weather, food and the beginning of driving. Weather plays such a large role in our lives when we travel. England was many things at many times. And great, of course, being able to communicate in our language. Now on to our next chapter, sunny Italy!

August 28, 2001 — Tuesday, 9:30 PM ROMA!

A new notebook—a new country. Right now I am feeling pretty low because we picked up the wrong suitcase at the airport and I don't know where ours is. It is the large duffel that contains all our clothes, gifts and odds and ends. I am really bummed. Our own fault as the luggage we picked up looks exactly like ours, and was next to our other two pieces on the carousel. I am waiting for a call from the airport. They have all our information and hopefully the bag is waiting in a room with unclaimed baggage. "We always have luggage issues," says Peter. Redundant. Yes.

ROMAN ADVENTURA

Everything went really well until now. We got out of the Heathrow hotel easily, cabbed to the airport, checked in and got on what turned out to be a very smooth and swift flight. We were met by a car and right away we knew we were in Italy, not just the language issue, but the visual differences. After a 45-minute drive we arrived at our apartment hotel and were delighted to find that this is the nicest long-term place we have stayed in yet.

We have two rooms, a separate small kitchen and a large terrace that has a view of a modern building and garden. The apartment is nicely and tastefully furnished. There is green fabric wallpaper that matches the green bedspread on our king size bed, blond wood furniture and a peach colored couch, dining room set, small yellow cabinet, and tables and nice lamps. We are pleased. We also have great closet space and shelves. I was feeling very up when we got here, we took a short walk and came upon a local and small Rinascente — a branch of the department store I frequented thirty years ago. We had a snack at the sixth floor's cafe, I was ECSTATIC to be in hot weather but now all my hot weather clothes are elsewhere. What more can I do or say. I just have to play a waiting game and pray for the best.

August 29, 2001 — Wednesday, 9:15 PM

I don't know what to make of today. First of all, we didn't get our luggage until 6 pm, so I wore the same black clothes for the third day and felt very hot. Either we're in England with such iffy weather or we're here where there is no doubt that not only it is very hot but it will stay this way. We slept well in this new place, which is extremely comfortable except that it is very dark. We even got an extra lamp. We keep walking into things and reading is difficult.

We had breakfast in the very pleasant dining room — cereal, bread, juice, stewed prunes, biscuits and coffee and tea. This place is very nice. The lobby is small and pretty, and from our large terrazzo we have a view into a very modern courtyard.

Peter and I left around 10 am and walked on the Via Veneto, which is just around the corner, to the Borghese Gardens. I remembered this street as being very special and we will see more of it later. It was hot in the park and we got to see the

Borghese Museum only on the outside. We walked through an underground tunnel from there to the Piazza di Spagna, the Spanish Steps. Brought back a lot of memories for me. I visited there when I was in my early twenties. Eons ago! Then on to American Express. "Peter! I remember exactly where American Express is!" More walking and saw Piazza di Popolo and some churches and took an electric bus. We went to GS, an underground supermarket, bought food and were frustrated because of the language. Decidedly, thus far, some, not most, people are not nearly as nice as the Parisians or the Brits. They seem impatient with us and are not very helpful.

We had a nice insalata at an outdoor cafe near American Express and saw lots of well-dressed ladies, and the inevitable beggars who are very pushy. The streets are jammed and have more motorcycles than I could count. This is a noisy, cluttered city. We planned on walking early before it gets too hot and then taking an American Express tour at 2:30 for four hours through old Rome. No way could we see all the city has to offer in the way of art, architecture and archeology in a few weeks.

Tomorrow is our fourteenth wedding anniversary, and we battled a lot today. Our agendas and priorities are so different right now. While on one hand we are "sightseeing out" I can't allow this jaded feeling to take over. I feel I must stir up the "awe" again. Domani.

August 30, 2001 — Thursday, 8 PM
HAPPY ANNIVERSARY TO US!

14 years of wedded bliss?

It is 8 pm and I am beyond pooped. I am looking around this apartment and realize I like that we can be in separate rooms even though it is just a wall really, put up to split a big room. We agree that some separation is good for both of us.

Anyway. Today. More events! Started out with an early breakfast at 7:45 am! We met a very nice American lady who works for the State Department and has, for the past thirty years, lived in many countries and likes South Africa the best. She is here for four months on assignment and is originally from Buffalo.

We left and walked to the internet place, which is about 20 minutes from this hotel. Rome is reputedly the noisiest city in Europe and I can believe this — all these motorcycles. The people are so-so. They are not so friendly and sometimes downright rude and bitchy. In Paris or London if we went into a shop to ask directions, people would actually walk outside with us to put us on the right path. Here, one lady in a shop where I made inquiries, said to me "this is not a tourist office." As we were walking, three kids came at us, one girl grabbing Peter's arm with her two hands, while another one tried to get at his money. Fortunately, a storeowner saw this, came out and shouted them away. Also, Peter yelled at them. Such, chutzpah! They had no fear of us whatsoever. I hold my purse tightly whenever I am around people, which is a lot of the time.

We then walked to the magnificent Trevi Fountain. So very beautiful it takes your breath away. And very touristy. We walked from there to the Pantheon. It is large and lovely and perfectly preserved. I remembered that when I first visited Rome when I was 23 or 24, a restaurant a friend and I frequented named Sagristia was near the Pantheon. I recalled that if I faced the Pantheon head on, the street of the restaurant would be on my left and nearest to the Pantheon. I took this route not really expecting the restaurant to still be there, but there it was! "Peter, it is quite updated and enlarged but there it is!" This was really thrilling to me. VERY. We went in and I talked to a man chopping vegetables who told me the same family owned it for the past 52 years. He worked there for the past 38 years, so it was quite possible he was there when I was! He looked to be a few years younger than me. I told him we would be back for dinner soon.

After a brief R&R in our hotel, back out again to Piazza di Spagna for our American Express tour. We had a few minutes to kill, so we walked Via Condotti, the most fashion wise street in Rome that has every store from Bulgari to Armani; all Italian designers, natch. The tour was great, but exhausting, as by now it is quite hot and we are walking on cobblestones. We saw old Rome, the Forum, temples, arches, lots of very ancient ruins and the topper, the colossal Coliseum that still today is breathtaking in scope and story. Our excellent guide told us all about the places we saw. It was truly a great and thoughtful tour. We also went to a church to see Michaelangelo's Moses. It was thrilling to see and know that he carved it from one gigantic piece of marble — the best marble, carrera, milky white.

We walked and bussed backed to Via Veneto and found a little pizzeria where we had pasta and wine. Via Veneto seems unduly quiet to me — I expected throngs of people on this, the most fashionable walking and eating street of the city. Tomorrow, I will venture forth on my own and visit the Excelsior that, all those years ago, was the top hotel in Rome. Sleep early and long, I hope! Buenasera. Buenanotte.

August 31, 2001 — Friday, 6 PM

We are sitting on our terrazzo, eating grapes and biscuits. There is a very nice breeze and the city has cooled considerably. We got a late start today. We met two women with small children in the breakfast room around 9:30 am. Both Americans, their husbands work in the military and one woman is going to be here for three years. They both lived in a lot of countries including Korea. The little boy Vaughn who is sixth months old sat on my lap. It felt wonderful. We left the apartment after noon and went to the internet. I got a few emails but wonder about all those I have sent, maybe people are away? I left Peter there and attempted to go to Garden Guirmale but after a long uphill walk found it to be closed and only open on Sundays. How weird is that?! Took a few turns down alleyways and ended up at Trevi.

Heard English being spoken in a small ristorante, and went in and ended up sitting with a couple from Philadelphia. We exchanged war stories about the Italians, they left and I had a really nice and sobering conversation with the manager, whose name is Tanni. She told me some truths about the Romans which explains their rudeness and feeling of superiority. Explains but does not excuse, I am thinking.

We have learned only to ask directions from policemen (others just lie), to be extremely careful of our money (which is very stressful), and never to make time a consideration. I told her we would be back for dinner and to see Trevi lit up.

I then went, via her good directions, to the Caraveggio exhibit at the Museo Nazionale, which was in the past, Mussolini's headquarters. The building was more awesome than the exhibit. There was a lot of great art, but just a few Caraveggios. Had I known I would have gone elsewhere. Then, I walked all the way back to our hotel getting a little lost at the end and spotted Peter on the street. We decided to eat on Via Veneto and saved Trastevere for tomorrow night when we have more daylight hours to walk around before dinner. I am feeling good about being here when, as always, we have plans.

September 1, 2001 — Saturday, 5 PM

I am in our room waiting for water to boil for tea. In four months and maybe ten places we have inhabited, this is the very first one where an electric teapot is not provided. Also, in every place in England, in the room was a tea service, tea, instant coffee, phony milk, sugar and biscuits and cookies. Here, I take the biscuits when I go to breakfast, back to the room. Peter is out at the market buying food for our Sunday picnic in a park, domani, which is Dominica. Tomorrow which is Sunday, that is.

It's been an awesome day. Rome doesn't seem to run out of ruins or monuments. We started out early as planned at 9:15 am after having breakfast separately. I am more than a little bored with the sameness of each breakfast, but hey — I don't have to prepare or clean after, which is a definite plus. We planned our day well and didn't get lost once. We took a bus nearby to the Victor Emmanuel monument, which is huge, white and mind- boggling. We climbed all the stairs to the top where we had a great view of the city.

Then, we climbed more stairs to Campodiglio or Capoltine Hill, which was where the capital of Rome was first housed. It was designed by Michaelangelo and has many buildings. Three weddings took place in a courtyard at the same time while we were there. Then we took a very long walk beside the Tevere, on the other side or Trastevere until we reached Piazza San Piatro. To the left was Vatican City, to the right was Castel Saint Angelo, the fortress and refuge of the Popes. We had a salad lunch at a nearby cafe and then opted for Castel Saint Angelo. We walked over 250 steps to the top and got the best view yet of the roof tops of Rome.

Inside was a museum showing how the Pope lives, even his bedroom. The ceilings of these rooms go back centuries and are still magnificent — almost like hieroglyphics. It took two busses to get us back and we saw something really wild. Outside the Castel, in the piazza, men were selling fake Louis Vuitton, Gucci and Prada purses. There were four or five men, their purses spread out on a sheet. Very suddenly, four of them gather up the sheet like a sack and start running down the steps to the river's bank, followed by two policemen! They ran at the speed of lightning. A bit later after the police disappeared, two of them came back! Actually, the purses were nice and I was considering buying one. Tonight, we are going to go to Piazza Navona and also see Trevi by night all lit up. Peter just told me that it has just started to rain! Good! The city is a lot cooler.

11 PM

Quite a pleasant evening. Left here around 6:15 or so and right on our street, Via Sicilia, started talking to two couples who were looking for a certain restaurant. Turns out they are from Granada Hills and Encino; small world department indeed. Got to

Trevi by bus and feet and was disappointed to find that Dickens, the restaurant where I wanted to eat, was closed. We ended up at a little restaurant near Trevi where we got an outdoor table. I just wanted fruit and cheese, which was on the menu but the owner said, "No, this is a restaurant, you will have to order meat. Cheese and fruits come after!" There was a sign in the restaurant that said "Salad is not a meal." Guess he told me. Got some ravioli and Peter had an omelet. A young couple from Cambridge, England, sat at a table next to us, and we ended up talking to them for our entire meal and after. They were so nice and so interesting. It is sad to me sometimes that we meet people and then we leave them knowing we will not see them again. We went to see Trevi lit up and unlike when we saw it during the day, the area was overcrowded and not inspiring at all. We walked to Piazza Navona, which knocked both of us out — so astounding in scope, size and beauty. The very large Piazza was filled with hundreds of people walking and talking. Cafes surround the Piazza. Is it like this every night or just on the weekend, I wonder?

September 2, 2001 — Dominica, 9 PM

Had dinner at a Chinese restaurant where the Chinese waiters spoke Italian.

I just turned on the TV and I am watching the beginning of "Casper, the Friendly Ghost" in Italian, I am that desperate. CNN is nothing but bad news over and over again. We picnicked in the park. We returned back to our apartment and decided not to go to Trastevere because Sunday everything is closed. We deliberated and ended up at the Piazza Republicca to see some sights. Lots of people there and some more ruins.

We had dinner at a Chinese restaurant and it was so-so. The waitress, who did not speak a word of English tried so hard to please, and she even gave me a Chinese tortoise plastic beaded bracelet. I was quite touched by this gesture. Found a homeopathic farmacia and the farmacist, a woman, spoke English and gave me something for a cold. Lights out, necessarily, by 10:30 pm. I keep hinting to Peter about returning to Paris for a week or two.

September 3, 2001 — Monday, 9:30 PM

So many thoughts. Just took a hot bath. It was an awesome day! Started out this am by bussing to Vatican City. We toured Saint Peter's Basilica and then I took a very long, five miles, three-hour tour to the museum that houses the Sistine Chapel. I can't put into words the feelings evoked in me upon seeing Michaelangelo's ceiling masterpieces, so I won't even try. After seeing so much beauty in France and England, I would have thought I would be jaded by now. Suffice to say I found this chapel beyond the belief of my being and astounding in every way. And one is not allowed to talk in the chapel. Good thing.

After a lunch nearby, we got on an electric big bus to who knows where and we went through a gorgeously rich area of Rome complete with huge Palazzos and then the bus took a turn and we ended up in the suburbs. I remembered this area because when I first was here many years ago, this is where I stayed, I think. Not sure which suburbs but they really all look alike with three to four story orange toned plain square apartment houses and the usual laundry hanging out the windows. Built post war. We walked around a bit and shared a cannoli. We took our very first metro. I was quite nervous regarding pickpockets but we were not in a tourist area so we were fine.

Had a glass of wine at a cafe on Via Veneto before going to take the #116 bus. We talked about the fact that some of the pizzazz was missing in Rome. Maybe we've just seen too much, maybe the locals neither nice nor friendly, maybe we have to be wary all the time, maybe all of the above or none of the above.

September 4, 2001 — Tuesday, 7:45

Peter is out at the internet place and I sort of half promised I would meet him, but after soaking in a very hot lavande bath, rinsing out a few things, eating a mixture of a half banana and some kind of lemon pudding, I am vegging out on a couch with CNN as company.

It was one of those days. We left here around 10 am. We went to American Express and a travel agency with dim results with regards to our plans for the rest of our trip. The Roman service people are the worst. They are rude, annoyed that you want them to actually do their jobs, curt, and generally quite disdainful of American tourists. We shared our first gelatti in a cone, sitting on the Spanish Steps.

I noticed that in most major cities we've visited there is one very large edifice where one sits on the steps and watches people. In New York City it's the Metropolitan Museum of Art, in Paris it's The Opera Garnier, and in Rome it's the Spanish Steps. Peter then went on to the railroad station where, he told me later, he waited on an endless line and got very little help. He said Italy really is a third world country. He was so frustrated he became exhausted, came home, and fell asleep at 3:30 pm.

I shopped around, bought two bras at Misses Robinson where I had to wait a half hour to try them on as the shop only had one dressing room. Had a late lunch at Dickens near Trevi and had a very nice conversation with Tanni. She helps me and tells me of interesting places to go and things to see. Walked Via del Corso and bought Peter two t-shirts and me a long sleeved one in blue. Back to the apartment via #116 bus by 5:30. Tomorrow we go to Trastevere and the Jewish section. Some of my aches and pains are gone. Weather much improved. Lifts my spirits.

September 5, 2001 — Wednesday, 8 PM

Just returned from a shared pasta dish and a glass of wine at a casual outdoor restaurant on Via Veneto. Did a lot of walking today, about 4 miles and thanks to having my pedometer fixed, I can now record my efforts. Left early around 9 am for Trastevere. Got a bus close by that took us practically to the doorsteps of the synagogue and Hebraica museum. We went to the small museum ourselves and then had a talk and a tour through the magnificent synagogue, which is about a hundred years old. We were pleasantly surprised to see how very palatial it is, complete with a dome very high up.

We found out that the architects were Christians, hence the church like feeling. The woman guide was very knowledgeable and told us all about the ghetto nearby. She lived in Rome throughout the war. She was a schoolgirl. We purchased two glass mezuzahs and promised to return for Friday night services; they also have Sephardic services in a small chapel. There are 16 temples throughout Rome; they are not independent but are all part of one synagogue organization. We walked through the ghetto, most of which is either gone or now upscale. We left there and walked and found a place for lunch on a busy street. The food was just awful.

After, we took a bus over the bridge to Trastevere and walked past Vatican City down into the heart of Trastevere where we stopped for a brief visit at a botanical garden, part of Villa Corsini.

Then even more walking near shops and restaurants, got a little lost, got a little tired and found an electric bus that took us near a place to take an actual bus into our neighborhood. Tomorrow we finalize plans for our next journey, see the Erte exhibit and if there is time, shop for shoes for Peter and a very necessary suitcase. There doesn't seem to be luggage stores here. In Paris there were three on each block. We will check out the department store, Rinascente nearby.

September 6, 2001 — Thursday, 9:30 PM

Just got in from a very unusual day. Nothing was as planned. Got out early and did emails, then went to a travel agent at 11:30 am. Worked with her until 1 pm when she closed for lunch, we are to return around 3 pm. Visited the Erte exhibit at Museo de Corso, which was very great, in a fabulous 1920's art deco setting. We loved his work, so jazzy and précise and boy did Erte love and idolize women. Had a quick bite at an outdoor cafe nearby and bussed back to the travel agency, our intention was to finish up with her, go back to the apartment for a rest and then return to the museum for a free jazz concert. It is 1920's American music, a tie in to the exhibit. We canceled our dinner plans. Well, we stayed at the travel agency until almost 6 pm and we still have to go back tomorrow to finish up. It got very complicated due, in part, to the fact that we couldn't find a place to stay in Sorrento or Ischia. Everything is booked and this stay will be for 5 days from now, so, without a rest or change of clothes, back to the museum and a quick bite there before the concert.

The concert was truly wonderful — four extremely talented jazz musicians. The curator of the exhibit was there so we went over to thank him and he spoke English and told us about the tie in of music each weekend with the exhibit. We chatted a while and he invited us to join him upon our return to Rome in October to see this jazz group at another venue. Then, he gave us a hardbound copy of the catalogue; a gorgeous book full of copies of the lithographs as a gift. We were stunned at his generosity. Right now I am about to wash some underwear for Peter. From the sublime to the ridiculous but necessary.

Our itinerary now is Rome, Naples, Vienna, Prague, Budapest, Milan, Venice, Florence and back to Rome. All by train. A blessing.

9 P.M Shabbat

Have to start with this evening and go backward because we had a stunning experience. We went to synagogue at 7 pm and to describe the feeling we both had could only be in one word — SPIRITUAL beyond anything I ever felt at a Jewish service of any kind on any holiday. It thrills me to think about it. At the synagogue, maybe a hundred men and fifty women drifted in at different times. The women sat high above in a balcony that has a great wall. I could barely see through it to the Bimah and the men below. The sounds were all Hebrew and no familiar melodies. Yet, I never felt so moved at a service in my entire life. I felt as if I was praying as the ancients did for thousands of years. I felt a kind of sadness afterwards, as if I had to give up something very special and too wonderful for words. I was completely high and completely low at the same time. We walked and bussed back to our place and did a great deal of talking about values, spirituality, Judaism, and Buddhism. As usual tired, but it is a weariness arising from this feeling of loss. We vowed to attend more synagogues in Europe on Friday nights and of course, the High Holidays are coming soon.

Earlier today, we went to Paola, our travel agent and finalized our plans. We were there over an hour. It was too late to visit the catacombs, which we'll do tomorrow, so we did a little bit of shopping for a suitcase and shoes. We had a late lunch at Dickens where Tanni works. I really like her a lot. Then back for a rest before going to the temple.

We both appreciate Rome now, more and more, especially after meeting nicer and friendlier people. Like Paris and in a way London, after ten days' time we can maneuver pretty well — busses and metros, which I really like as the metros all have escalators being so deep in the ground. The weather is A+ warm and sunny and not too hot. Rome is very beautiful in many ways and we feel the presence of ghosts of ancient Rome all the time, especially when we walk Steep Street. Peter says it's in these areas that another civilization existed under the streets. We see ruins everywhere and it is quite eerie. We can learn a lot from just walking and listening. Traffic is a horror.

A motorcycle backed into me as I was crossing the street. No apologies. It is very dirty here and there is a blend of the nicest and the nastiest people. Today we found an open-air market, bought two peaches, sat on a park bench and enjoyed it so much. BUENASERRA.

September 8, 2001 — Saturday, 6 PM

Still high about last night's events.

Wonders will never cease! Today at about 11 am while awaiting to enter the catacombs at San Calisto, outside of Rome, a woman sees me and shrieks! It was Agnes, Margie's daughter in law's mother and her husband Eric, her sister Alma and a cousin, they are all visiting in Rome. I am still in shock. What fate conspired to bring us together?! "I heard your voice, but was unsure it was you because I didn't recognize Peter with his beard." Agnes knew we were in Rome via Margie. It is so GREAT seeing someone from home and not just a passing acquaintance. We chatted after the tour through the catacombs, which was mind boggling — so many thousands of burial plots, five stories of this. It was a bit claustrophobic but fascinating nonetheless. We were graciously invited to Sunday afternoon dinner in San Calisto by Agnes' relatives and we accepted. We got there by bus, metro, walking and yet another bus, about an hour total travel time. On the final bus which also goes to Appia Antica, the oldest road in Rome built in 312 BC!! — there was a bunch of tourists from Spain, we got to talk with them and one man is originally from Bejar which is the town of my ancestors before they fled to escape the Inquisition in 1492. I've learned on this trip to talk to every one as often as possible. It is amazing what you find out.

Another example of this is Carol, a lady whom we met at our hotel. We see her at breakfast and she helps our logistic issues. She put me on to a beauty salon and just a few hours ago I had my first pedicure since leaving the US and my first manicure since late June. I feel cleaner, neater and I don't cringe when I look at my hands. We planned on going to Sagristia tonight but we just too tired to go that far and eat a big meal, so we are going to a local "real" family Italian restaurant that appeals to Peter. Hope to do Sagristia in October when we return to Rome after our excursion. We walked 2.65 miles today — not a lot — but a lot in the heat!

September 9, 2001 — Sunday, 6 PM

Just got in, plopped myself down on a couch and turned-on CNN. Peter is at the Internet place. I was there for a bit but became so frustrated because of all the problems involved with sending the email. I don't think any of them are getting through.

We had dinner last night at the family restaurant nearby. Everyone spoke English as they were from the US, Ireland, England or Australia! We told the owner we don't eat meat and brought us out a great meal of grilled veggies, a whole small trout each broiled to perfection and fresh fruit salad topped with a little pistachio ice cream and of course vino.

Today we went out to Agnes' cousin for dinner way out in the country. Or so it seemed. When we got off the bus on the street to which we were directed, we didn't know where to go; we didn't get an exact address. We started wandering around and people found us, knew who we were, and guided us to the right apartment house building.

Word gets around. The food kept coming! It was a 20 minutes taxi ride out to the suburbs from the bus stop. Maria is so sweet, she insisted on driving us back. All the family was so nice, hospitable and generous. Very loving. I noted that the men do not help at all during the meal. After he was finished eating, even though the rest of us were at the table, Maria's husband got up, walked past the kitchen and turned on a TV. I wondered why he didn't bring his dishes into the kitchen. He was quite a nice man and told me before I could (or would!) ask that he goes to work and Maria takes care of the house. End of sentence. Evidently Margie already knows about our chance meeting with Agnes, because Agnes phoned David and

David will tell Margie. She will flip out! Tonight, no dinner, we are stuffed and we'll maybe take a short walk.

September 10, 2001 — Monday, 9 PM

I am sitting in the midst of chaos. We are preparing to leave Rome and it has taken all day. Started out doing laundry this morning and had to taxi both ways due to the heaviness of the laundry and the distance. Later, we went out for a quick pizza lunch and back to the apartment to the ironing. Then, separating what we are taking from what we are leaving here was not an easy decision! Out for an ice-cream break on Via Veneto where it is classier than ever. After more packing, dinner at Jasmine, the local Chinese restaurant. For quite a while we were the only customers, the food was just so- so but red wine is a great equalizer. Now, finishing up the packing and tomorrow we leave for Naples. I am leaving my diaries behind and don't feel good about this. Tried for the third time to send a group email to no avail. I was pissed — all the time and energy for naught. Oh well. Maybe there will be a theater in Naples with English speaking movies. Peter says we will check for this right away! Yippee.

NAPLES

September 12, 2001 — Wednesday, 9:45 AM
Naples AFTER HORRIFIC 9/11.

I had no desire to write anything yesterday due to the HORRIFIC concurrencies in New York and DC. It was 5:30 pm in Naples where we are so it was 11:30 am in New York when we heard the news about the bombings. We were stunned. We left Rome for Naples yesterday and after some delays traveled quite comfortably on a train for less than two hours to arrive in Naples. I met a gentleman in Stazioni Termini who spoke French and helped us get our tickets. I bought him a cafe au lait (cappuccino here.) After a 45-minute cab ride we got to our hotel, high up on a hill overlooking one side of Naples and we have a distant view of the bay. At first, I hated the hotel because it has no charm and is very bare bones, but now I find it OK as in the sunlight we have a fantastic view from our balcony. This is definitely not geared to Americans. Even CNN is only in Italian.

We must travel by cab or funicular which is sort of a cable car that starts on the ground and goes up and down a steep hill to the Bay of Naples; this bay is on the other side of our hotel. We got to the bottom and passed a very upscale residential area. We checked out all the dock areas to find out about boats to Ischia, Capri, etc. We then went to a tourist office to check out other hotels and all were booked. We would like to be closer to the water but unless we want to pay a lot it's not possible.

THAT'S when we heard the awful news from a travel agent who spoke little English. She kept saying "Finished. Gone. Twin buildings. Finished gone." We didn't want to believe it. We fervently hoped we heard her wrong. From there we went for a drink at a local café where the English speaking waiter told us further news from the American Embassy. There were dozens of police, all armed. Went back to our hotel and walked down to the Hotel Paradise, a lovely four- star hotel (and very near us –I wanted to stay there) to watch CNN in English and to have dinner. We somehow picked up (or she picked us up) an American tourist from New York and took her to the hotel with us. It seems that her apartment is across from the World Trade Center and she is fearful that it is gone. We watched for hours. Her cat was in the apartment. She was hoping to get out of Naples as soon as possible.

Today we plan on going back to Hotel Paradise to see a news up-date and then just hanging out: we are too somber to do much else. I pray for those who have suffered this terrible calamity.

6:30 PM Same day

Sitting on our balcony, warm sun, view of rooftops and Bay of Naples. We're on the fourth floor and quite a bit higher than sea level. We climbed a steep hill from street level to enter our hotel. Today we were very quiet but amazingly enough did not think of the situation in New York all the time, I don't think it has hit us yet. After breakfast we went to the Hotel Paradise and watched about an hour of CNN. We also made phone calls. I got through to Marjorie in New York at 5 am her time. She is of course very sad and she says the city is in shock and everyone is home and glued to the TV. The phone call cost $ 16 American but was worth it. We walked downhill into town and it was so beautiful and tranquil by the Bay, you 'd never know of the horrors in the US. We can't get enough of CNN; the foreigners in the hotel don't seem to care.

We took a bus ride around Napoli. It is the noisiest city I've ever been in my life, mostly from thousands of cars and motorcycles racing by. People drive so fast and the cars are so close to each other there must be many, many accidents. We got out at Piazza Vittorio and walked bayside down, stopped at a trattoria for lunch, which was an omelet and salad and then walked to the funicular, stopping at Hotel Paradise for more news. We finally saw Bush talk and also Hilary. Then we found a market and bought some fruit for later as we have a small fridge in the room. Tomorrow we will go to Ischia by hydrofoil, hopefully. I can hear the din of traffic even though we are far above it.

Naples. Dirty, crowded, noisy, and earthy. The bay is beautiful but we haven't seen anything lovely yet, i.e. shops, hotel, scenery, museums. We are on the edge of an upscale neighborhood but downtown Naples seems bleak, old and decrepit. It has some charm in its naturalness and not giving into urban renewal, but I don't find this a place to stay. We will use this place to rest in between our boat trips to other places. The people are nice enough but no one speaks English. I think if they do they will leave here for Rome or other cities.

There is garbage everywhere and cars parked on the sidewalk, which makes walking awful. Laundry hangs from every window. We are comfortable in this hotel but I wouldn't recommend it. It is very plain with few amenities. A dog came up to me and I petted it. I am so lonesome for my Lucy.

September 13, 2001 — Thursday, 6 PM

Our son telephoned from Los Angeles at 6:30 am full of doom and gloom and said we should come home right away. I said "Why? We are safe here." Arose and took the 10:30 ferry (hydrofoil, 45 minutes) to Ischia Forio. We arrived at a very sunny and pleasant place, which is much larger than we thought it would be.

A bus takes us to a spa/resort called Poseidon Thermal, which was recommended to us. It is very large, on the beach front and extends back to a mountain, has several levels with maybe 15 pools, 10 which are thermal. Fabulous. The pools are filled with mineral waters in different temperatures, ranging from 32 C to 40 C which is very hot. I loved it! Mostly Germans are here, and all are fat. Really fat. Heard a lot of German spoken, and in the restaurant where we are served a cafeteria-style lunch there were many German dishes and lots of beer. We hung around several pools and I even got to sit on a "Rock Chair" while water cascaded down on to me. It was such fun. Then a visit to the beach. "I can now say I swam in the Bay of Naples," Peter proclaims. We sat on old-fashioned canvas beach chairs and had a large straw umbrella to shelter us from the sun. The place is very beautiful and if I lived nearby, I would go there a lot. We left to walk around a bit before getting the last ferry at 7:30 back. Took a detour to the Paradise Hotel to see CNN's update. So grim and sad. I may be flying solo tomorrow as Peter wants to go into town center and do internet stuff. Right now I am too tired to consider the one hour bus trip each way.

Thursday, 8 PM — Alone in the room

Peter is at the internet. I just got back from being there and it's a horrid dirty place. I walked down Via Toledo, a big shopping street, caught the R3 bus. Children sit and their parents stand. No comment necessary.

A day of exasperation, the Neapolitans are nicer than the Romans but more stupid and much less efficient. Spent several hours this morning looking for the synagogue, which is nearby, but not close enough to walk. We will go there on Rosh Hashonah which is Tuesday. We thought it was Monday and Tuesday and we will travel on Monday, now this means we'll be traveling on the second day of Rosh Hashonah. The temple is large outside and small inside; it is part of a villa given to the Jewish community by the Rothschild family. We met, among others, an American woman carrying her three-month baby on her chest. The baby's name is Eliana. The lady lives in Naples and works for Price Waterhouse in London. She was very nice and helpful to us. Also there was a young Jewish man on tour from New York. He extolled the virtues of Napoli which I have yet to find, but he was talking about the museums and churches which we might not even see. We will see this Jewish woman at services.

We walked and found ourselves in the nicest and richest shopping area of Naples and after much difficulty we found the tourist office. They weren't very helpful, giving us a mass of misinformation. We found our way by bus, thanks to an English-speaking salesgirl to the Piazza Dante where we were to find English language books. The area was flooded with bookstores but all Italian and mostly school textbooks. We went into one bookstore and picked up three books by an author I've never read. Peter and I fought about taking taxis vs. busses. It is my contention that when you need to go somewhere specific and you only have a vague idea of where it is, you take a cab. Easy. Fast. Not tiring. Peter feels differently. And so it goes.

I found a newsstand that had one copy of a magazine in English, Elle, for almost five dollars. I grabbed it! Tomorrow we go to Capri. Tonight, the gossip in Elle! But mosly prayers for NYC and Washington, DC.

September 14, 2001 — Saturday, 8 PM

Well, the best laid plans ... We awoke at 2 am to very loud thunder and very bright lightning. I can honestly say that neither of us ever heard nor saw anything like this in our lives. Loud and scary thunder and bright lightning for a few hours and pouring rain.

We couldn't sleep and got out of bed in the morning quite groggy. We canceled our plans to go to Capri even though the sun was now shining as we felt the boat ride would be rough and Capri would be wet. Instead, we went to Museo Nazionale, which is architectural and has an amazing exhibit of Greek and Romans statues, artifacts and frescos preserved for 2000 years under the volcanic ashes of Pompei. We started out for the funicular only to find it wasn't working due to the storm. After a very long wait for a bus that didn't come, we walked down to Hotel Paradise to get a taxi.

Napoli is filthy. There is no getting away from this fact. The streets are strewn with litter, there is dust everywhere, the cars and motorcycles emit dreadful smoke and make so much noise, the streets are torn up and stay that way, the steps and buildings are decaying, and no one seems to care. There is no respect for order here, as well. Most of people are quite nice, but seem oblivious to what I call urban blight.

After a pasta lunch we went, finally, to see the 4- and 5-star hotels facing the water. There are about 6 of these and they are large and sumptuous, beautiful and definitely stand out because they are so different from the other buildings. I would have liked to stay in one of them. We went in a few and it was such a great relief! Aesthetics and comfort are so important to me. After, we took a long walk by the water and had a heart-to-heart talk about the future. We had to take a taxi back to our hotel because the funicular was still not working. Peter said it probably won't be fixed until after we leave. We're both tired and had dinner in the room. We will read and go to bed early. I can't believe I am watching "The Mask of Zorro" dubbed in Italian. It is probably 40 years old. We are both so desperate for TV or a movie to relax with. We talked about our burn out and the fact that we really don't want to run to museums or monuments but care more about hanging out and letting the city into our consciousness.

September 16, 2001 — Sunday, 8 PM

There are only moments now of really feeling high and excited about the places we visit. Unsettling, yes, but it's my truth, at least right now. Everything here in Naples takes so much work. We left by cab for the ferry to Capri. It was a rough but short ride, as the weather was so- so and the water choppy. When we got there, we encountered hundreds of people on the shore and many dozens tourist shops and places to eat. We met two girls from Dublin and took a cab ride with them up to Ana Capri. It, too, was very crowded with shops, even Armani, Ferragamo, as well as the usual touristy junk. We had a lovely lunch there and I bought some little gifts and a pair of shoes. We took a nice walk down an old road right along the bay and only partially succeeded in getting away from people. We hung out a bit and then took a hair raising mini-bus ride down a steep road to Capri Center. I had my eyes closed the entire time. We went to see the Gardens of Augustus and the views were extraordinary. Then, walking through lots of people, we found steps leading down to the dock where we came in now filled with seemingly thousands of people. I hated it. I just can't stand crowds anymore. But I like to talk to people. Go figure.

We took a ferry back, walked forever to a MacDonalds and then took a taxi back up to our place. Everything in Naples is crowded, fast, and noisy and it's very risky just crossing the street. The moments of genuine enjoyment today were few. I liked Ischia a whole lot better. As Peter puts it "We've seen so much we just don't get excited much anymore." I think this is a real shame. I want to look forward to Vienna et al, especially considering all the discomfort and inconveniences we've had to endure. Of course, we are both very down now due to the events in NYC and DC.

September 17, 2001 — Monday, 11 PM

Just returned via a rip off cab ride from Hotel Paradise where we watched CNN and had Rosh Hoshana dinner; certainly a nice but lonely holiday meal. The view is lovely and the crowd lively. We hadn't an easy day, due in part to our both being sleep deprived. We took a stroll a bit beyond the neighborhood and did errand shopping. Then back for a lunch of cornflakes, a short rest and a bus trip ride — C27. Just so so. Naples is so decayed looking it is hard to enjoy the site. Peter and I actually can't wait to leave here. Tomorrow we go to synagogue. LA CHANA TOVA.

September 18, 2001 —
Tuesday, 6 PM ROSH HOSHANAH

We're back in the room, having left at 9 am to go to temple. We stayed until about noon or so, I think? Maybe later. I had mixed feelings about temple. Glad to partake in the holiday, sad that I knew no one and all the woman knew each other, and sad to not be among friends. I did see the young woman and the baby whom we befriended. It was actually bitter sweet to see her knowing we will never see her again. She is one person I would have liked to get to know. We took a walk among the chic shops — this is really only one long block of them and they are all Italians — Gucci, Armani, Ferragamo, Monti, Bulgari and a few others. We had a simple lunch at a charming restaurant at the area overlooking the bay. Then we took a bus that took us through about 90 minutes of stunningly awful areas full of commercial buildings, docks, and all were gritty and ugly. We were practically in the countryside when we got out and returned to the dock area. We ate ice cream and discovered on our very last day here a whole lineup of cafés and pizzerias facing the water. Our hotel manager is not helpful in anyway and never tells us anything. We took our last funicular ride up. Soon I'll start packing. We both agree we've been here too long.

September 19, 2001 — Wednesday, 5 PM ROME!

We're in a restaurant way in the corner with our luggage on a cart. Peter went to exchange money for Austria. The restaurant is in a Terminal; we left our hotel around noon and arrived so early we decided to take the 1:30 pm train to Rome rather than wait for the 3:30. This works if you're willing to give up your reserved seat and just sit anywhere. We did and came across two American couples, one from Valencia, CA and the other from Vegas. They had horror stories about Palermo. The Italians here are something else. We didn't get ripped off by our cab driver but when we tried to get our stuff on a train, a man helped us, whether we wanted him to or not. We didn't. We give him 500 lira anyway. He turned this down and demanded 1000. We said NO — take this or leave it. He took it.

I am apprehensive about the train to Vienna. We got on a night train and have a private compartment. There are stories about how these trains are attacked at night by thieves who send gas under the door to your compartment and then rob you while you sleep. We are told to sleep with our passports near our bodies. All worry was for nothing, it was a lovely ride through mountains and going through snow. We slept in bunk beds, Peter on top with netting to keep him from falling out. We awoke in the middle of the night as the train made a stop and we heard it. We looked out and saw tons of snow. It was magical. Later in the morning, we had our breakfast, ordered the night before, in our compartment. Both of us think about Washington and NYC a lot. We are fearful.

I look at myself in the mirror and realize how much maintenance I need! My nails are a mess, could use a facial and massage and my clothes are a wreck. The saving grace is that no one knows me here, but I've come to realize that's not it. It is all about how I look to myself. On another note Peter says we can't buy one more thing because our bags are bursting and getting too heavy. Can I really go to places I've never been and not buy anything? I think not.

VIENNA

September 20, 2001

Last night we boarded the train around 6:45 pm. We had the cutest compartment. In fact, it was possible to sleep three, one above another. We had a large picture window, a sink with a wooden top, medicine cabinet with soap, towels, razors, a few hooks and hangers, a luggage rack and a couch that seats three and then opens up to a bed. We tried sleeping together in the bottom bunk but not roomy enough. Peter slept on top held in place by the large net.

We met a young couple that assured us we would not be gassed because our compartment locked from the inside. I was not reassured. I did sleep very well until 3:10 am when the train made a stop. Before we went back to sleep, we saw the train stop at Orvieto and Firenze. The train twisted and swayed and went very fast. I enjoyed all the rocking. We went through some mountain passes and a tunnel. Peter and I awoke around 6 am and Peter joined me in the lower berth as we watched the passing scenery. It was a fairy land. Peter kept saying "We're in Austria, we're in Austria!" This is the city of his birth and so very exciting for him to be here. We got to our Hotel Savoy early, around 9:30 a.m. Our room is very enchanting and very old Viennese. It is spacious and has a large walk-in closet and thankfully! A bathtub that is huge. We went out right away and had a strange breakfast where they charged Peter 2 s (15 cents) for milk, for his tea and it was a thimbleful. We walked a very modern upscale shopping area to the Opera. Got tickets and Peter is dreading it. The Viennese Opera House is a dream of a place and somewhere I want to go. Came back and unpacked, bathed and went out again to find PETER'S CHILDHOOD HOME. This was very emotional for him. We took several metros already; they are very clean and all have escalators and elevators!

Vienna is, at first glance, incredibly immaculate and orderly. People don't push or jump into traffic — such a pleasure. I feel safe here. Weather cooler but not cold, sweater weather. The clothes I see on the streets are divine. The women look the best groomed and most fashionable I've seen yet in Europe. Of course, these are fall/winter clothes and I've not seen that anywhere else. I feel like an absolute slob. Everyone speaks English. It is easy to be here. I was ready to be defensive in Austria but see that there is no need. Everyone is incredibly nice, but I can't help wondering... where were the parents and grandparents during the war. How many were Nazis or merely closed their eyes to what was happening.

Naples was just awful and, in the end, it was a dirty mad house with people ripping us off everywhere. Now in an immaculate Vienna, tomorrow we will take a hop on up off bus. Peter is absolutely not going to take a guided tour for quite a while!

September 21, 2001 — Friday, 7:40 pm

Somewhere around this time we visited the building that was Peter's childhood home.

Peter was about 2 years old when his mother, his uncle and he started to flee Europe. He says he remembers the building and the yard where his mother played with him. There is a church across the street that was there when Peter lived in the neighborhood. A very emotional experience for him.

I was groggy and tired all today. Left here at 2:30 pm and took a hop on hop off bus for 3 hours. Saw a lot of old and new Vienna but did not hop off. We purchased a 2-day ticket and will use it to go to The Schoenbrunn Palace, which has 1400 rooms, zoological gardens and beautiful gardens. 1400 rooms!

The sun is out to almost 10 pm. Have to study about Vienna until then. Watched "Murder She Wrote" dubbed in German. I will attempt to look halfway decent tomorrow. My morale is low.

September 22, 2001 — Saturday, 10:30 PM

Today was filled with an unhappy circumstance that led to an extremely happy one. As planned, we took a bus to the Imperial Palace at Schoenbrunn which was the home of the Hapsburgs for centuries, and where Franz Joseph and his child bride reigned for many years until he died. Upon entering a magnificent lemon-yellow building of 1440 rooms! 40 of which are open to the public, we decided to use the ATM machine inside because inexplicably a lot of businesses don't take credit cards, this museum being one of them. The ATM machine "took" my card and said "transaction cancelled" and kept my card! We got hold of a bigwig at the palace who tried to help us but could only give us the address of the bank, which, of course, is closed until Monday. In passing he mentioned a ONCE-A-YEAR EVENT that was going to take place at the palace that night. It is called "FEST IM SCHLOSS SCHOENBRUNN" starting at 6:30 pm and ending at 11 pm, featuring music played in several of the great palace halls. You go from one room to the other and the concerts are repeated in case there are two things going on simultaneously that you want to see. We experience: a marionette show backed by an orchestra in the greatest hall of all, a concert in the chapel, a flutist and harpist in Rose Zimmer Hall and maybe three or four more. IT WAS FABULOUS – a once in a lifetime experience. We've had a few of these, I am thankful to say. But this was the grandest. We left at 10 pm very exhilarated. And -- had we not had the mishap with the credit card, we never would have known about this great event.

Right now, I have "Father of the Bride" on the telly with Steve Martin and Diane Keaton speaking German. Peter says he could stay in Vienna another week past our departure date and I agree with him, maybe we'll do it? Go right from here to Prague! It's an idea!

September 23, 2001 — Sunday, 4 PM

Hot hot bath. This is becoming a necessary afternoon routine. This the best bath yet, heats up quickly, full force and I can jump into it within minutes. Today we were sent on a fool's errand. We attempted to go the Lichtenstein Palace because according to our guide books, that is where the German Expressionism and modern arts is. We were supposed to take the U2 metro and then a tram. We found that the tram wasn't running because a marathon was being run on the street, on the main ring in Vienna. So, in true Peter fashion, we walked. And walked. Got lost. Went in the Hilton Hotel where a very kind concierge helped us. It seems that all the arts have been moved to the new Leopold Museum, in museum quarters and just opened yesterday. We walked to the Landslann, which is the most famous restaurant/cafe in Vienna. It is 125 years old and was frequented by Freud among other greats. Had kaffee mit shlag and chokolat there, took a subway to the Leopold Museum. Rain starting. Had a very nice time. The museum is brand new and ultra-modern. Part of the great exhibits included works by the artist Egon Schiele. Peter and I were so impressed we bought a book about him and several notebooks with his art on the cover to give as gifts.

Tonight, we go to the Opera. We are hungry, there is no food here and the markets are closed. We are really too tired for a restaurant and would just as soon nibble in the room. I am going to start a John Grisham book. The Barbara Taylor Bradford was so simplistic and predictable. I can't believe she sells millions of books but she does. More aprés l'Opera, mes amis.

Opera was a terrible experience, save for seeing the magnificent building. Wagner was way too long; seats were so so and we could barely read the English translation of the music. And no intermission. We left half way through. Peter didn't want to go to begin with; I felt badly that he had to suffer this ordeal.

September 24, 2001 — Monday, 10 PM Futility.

Can't get my ATM card back. It will be cut in half. It seems the bank back home issued new cards (mine should be in the mail when I get home) and discontinued the one I tried to use. Took us four hours to find the proper agent to get Peter 's birth certificate and the agency turns out to be 2 subways stop away, or a good but easy walk.

Visited a local internet venue. Fabulous and modern place. I attempted to send a group message and I doubt if it went through and I did it twice.

Attempted to phone Joseph, not home. Henry not home. Phoned Margie and it was good to chat.

Visited two Jewish museums today after which we had a fish dinner at a restaurant at Stephansplatz, a large promenade in the middle of city with shops, restaurants, and a big church. This is an area I've gotten to love.

Did futile internet, came back and washed a ton of laundry in the bathtub. Peter is still at the internet place. I lost another diamond from my ring. This makes three. Don't quite know what to make of our stay in Vienna. So far it's been highly emotional. And it's so beautiful here. I wish we could stay longer. I like it here more and more and don't like this feeling of getting to know and like a place and then having to leave, as I've stated before, you will notice. Tomorrow we plan on going to the Freud Museum and just walking around the city.

September 25, 2001 — Tuesday, 9:30 PM

Tomorrow we leave Vienna. Boohoo. Don't want to go. Just when we found our places it is time to go which has been true about a lot of our trip.

Today was good. We took it easy. Went to the Freud Museum in the morning by subway and tram and didn't get lost! It was very very interesting. I really felt Freud's presence. He had a very large apartment and offices in an upscale neighborhood. We saw the famous couch which is roped off. It's in great condition. I am not surprised. Afterwards, we took a tram (electric bus) ride to an area called Greizig to the entrance of the famous Vienna woods. This area is right out of a storybook about Vienna, old with pastel buildings and beer halls. I expected to see waiters in lederhosen singing German songs. Had desserts there and took a tram back into the inner ring. Walked around in very mild weather, no rain today.

Visited some ultra-fashionable shops and bought myself a gorgeous mohair sweater, expensive, but with the VAT not all that bad. It's stunning and it picked me up, I've been feeling dowdy lately. We kept walking and lo and behold, right into and through the royal Palace, another unbelievable complex of fabulous palatial buildings and parks. The Hapsburgs had it good! Back to the hotel for rest and the start of packing. Got a new TV in the room that gets CNN. Ironic. Our last day and we finally got CNN in English. Went to dinner at La Boheme on the most charming cobblestone street ever. And no cars. Back to continue packing and watched more CNN. We leave here 9 am tomorrow.

BUDAPEST and PRAGUE

September 26, 2001 — Wednesday, 7PM
Budapest — Eve of Yom Kippur

We need to make our prayers soon so I may have to cut this short. We are allowing ourselves only reading and sleep.

Our train ride was pleasant. We met a New Yorker named Linda Miller who visited her daughter in London for Rosh Hashanah and is now visiting her son who lives in Budapest for Yom Kippur.

It was sad saying goodbye to Isabella at the front desk of the Savoy in Vienna. We meet people we like and know will not see them again. Am I being redundant? Still the truth.

We arrive in Budapest around 1 pm. On the train, there were two sets of very young military people, one from Austria and the other from Hungary sternly checking our passports on the train. Very serious types. The train station looks like a scene from a pre-war movie —old, decaying but with a grandeur. Very primitive. It took a half hour to get our train ticket from Budapest as all arrangements are done by hand, no computer. The porter and the cab driver waited around for us. I felt badly for them. The porter made about 5 dollars and the cab driver about 20 dollars.

The hotel in Budapest is very modern and the room is completely filled with the king size bed, a desk and TV. Ironically, the one night of the year I don't watch TV they have English speaking movies to rent on TV. This is a definite for Friday night!

We dropped our stuff off, had a quick lunch and then took off to see Budapest. One side of the Danube is Buda and the other is Pest. Peter thinks we're on the Buda side. We are very near the Danube so we walked over a long and old magnificent bridge to the other side. It was more thrilling than I would have imagined. The old and new part of the city all coming together. We went into what appeared to be the upscale "Fifth Avenue" street; the Opera is there as well as cafes, boutiques. Peter actually changed money with a guy on the street and got a great rate. I remember an "I love Lucy" episode like this and she got arrested for passing counterfeit money! We got some wine, bread and flowers in observance of Yom Kippur. Tomorrow we go to the "big" shul which is the grand one. Hopefully there will be no problem in getting in.

May we all live safe, sane and healthy lives in the New Year. PEACE AMEN

NAMASTE

September 27, 2001 — Thursday, 8 PM Yom Kippur

Had a small stomach bout last night. Many roll aids and a xanax wiped it and me out. Scary. These bouts seem to come in groups. Went to sleep early and stayed in bed until 10 am. I dressed quickly, no bath and of course no food, so off we went by cab to the big shul. Turns out this is the largest synagogue in Europe, second only to the one in Jerusalem. It is huge and seats over 2000 congregants and has two large U-shaped wrap around balconies. The style is mosaic, middle-eastern and somewhat church like. There was a large choir, heard but not seen. Many rabbis and cantors on the bimah. Lots of talking among the attendees. Definitely not orthodox! Peter and I sat together on a side aisle up seat. We were told that Tony Curtis donated $IM to the temple. Tony, or should I say Bernie Schwartz, is Hungarian. After a few hours we left to walk around and ended up at the shopping area near the water. Most pleasant. We sat at a park facing the Danube. Hard to believe! Such a famous river and we walked over it by bridge twice. Took a rest, broke the fast, and then went right across the street to a coffee house where we had open faced tuna sandwiches and bowls of hot tea. Tomorrow is a full day; a three hour-tour in the morning, shopping and then thermal bath later. And maybe dinner out. I wish I had more initiative to do night life. Synagogue was strange for me. I felt unfulfilled and in strange territory, but then again that's where I am. Budapest is an intriguing city and this visit is all too short. Just a small bite of a piece of delicious cake.

September 28, 2001 — Friday, 8:30 PM

Boy! Do I have a lot to say. I am just a little bit tipsy and I want to write while still high. And see what comes out.

This hotel is nice enough. Plain and ultra-modern, nicely boring and contains 74 units. The best breakfast we've had yet eggs scrambled or boiled, three kinds of bread, vegetables, cooked fruits, juices, coffee, cereals. Lots of tables full of lots of tourists. However, the concierge definitely doesn't want to be here and treats us with disdain and gives erroneous information. We took his advice on which three-hour tour to take this morning (assuredly there is a kick back involved) and it didn't go past the synagogue which is a place we wanted to take pictures. And then the biggie. Went to the famous Gellord Bath and were assured by our concierge that a swimsuit was not needed as you can rent one there. I was told that I could have a massage without an appointment. Neither was true.

Eddie Murphy is here filming "I Spy" and the better part of Buda, where we are staying is in chaos. Roads and bridges are closed, equipment everywhere. He is staying at the Gellord. The day was a good one. The tour was A+ and the tour guide, a feisty lady was great and a real pisser. We saw the highlights and the castle area, which is a healthy but walkable distance from us. It is quite spectacular. At 1 pm we had lunch at a cafe on the Pest side facing the Danube, it is a warm and sunny day. Really nice. While in the area we did some tourist shopping, gifts for the kids and grandkids then on to the Gellord Bath which has to be seen to be believed, enormous, old Roman bath like.

October 1, 2001 — Monday, 8 PM

Another busy day with less structure and more flow. Went back to the castle to see the church, walked a bit and then took our stroll through Mala Strana one of the nicest areas with big squares, old beautiful buildings, the usual! Had lunch at the big square at City Center, probably the most happening square in the city with lots of shops, restaurants, and tourists with a few sensationally gorgeous churches surrounding. I am running out of superlatives. We walked over the Charles Bridge and this so reminded me of Paris, left and right banks. The shoreline is to die for, a storybook group of fantasy buildings.

Walked into the main shopping area and did some errands. Went to a food market and noted that all the large markets in Europe are underground. Good planning. Took the metro back. The metros here are so deep into the ground that the escalators go twice as fast as anywhere else. We plan on a boat ride tomorrow, weather permitting (it has rained partially today and yesterday), internet and TA DA! A movie late afternoon or early evening. I'll see anything in English or even with English subtitles.

I am nervous in the early morning. I am tired of washing clothes in the sink and having them strewn around the room. Hate the way I look. Understandable and to be expected. It's 150 days since we left home. Yikes! Better demain! Miss Paris.

PRAGUE

October 2, 2001 — Tuesday, 11 PM

We just returned from seeing "Bridget Jones Diary" for the second time. We took a metro to an area called Seme Most and it was really far, at least half hour on the metro plus a huge walk. It seems to be a very new area, definitely the suburbs, tall skyscrapers, gigantic shopping mall and a very modern multiplex. Started to see "The Fast and the Furious," a movie which, in a 5-minute period, proved to be violent, noisy and dumb to us. The only other movie at that time worth seeing was "Bridget Jones Diary." Peter hadn't seen it, so there we went. I am very disappointed. Travel 2 hours round trip to see a movie I've already seen.

Went out around 10:30 heading to the Internet place where I stayed two hours and 21 minutes. Lots of mails from friends, all doom and gloom, which made me depressed. Then, there was an email from my cousin Henry regarding the possibility of a temporary furnished apartment for 2 to 3 months in the Marina. Phoned the party and Henry (great to hear his voice) and now we shall see.

Had a lovely lunch at an outdoor restaurant in the main square. Weather is excellent today and we wore heavy clothes and even took an umbrella, all for nought.

October 3, 2001 — Wednesday, 9 PM

Watching "Shawshank Redemption" in German. Peter flossing his teeth and I can't listen to the plinking. Well! Our plans have changed. We are leaving tomorrow at 3 pm for Vienna! I happened to look at our tickets for the overnight train to Venice and was shocked — shocked! to find we are not leaving from Prague for Venice but from Vienna, so we decided to go to Vienna early. I am glad about this as I like Vienna a lot and will now have 2 and half days there, in the same lovely hotel, the Savoy. Prague is OK, but eight days is too much.

Today, after many phone calls to California, we are so happy to get the temporary rental in the Marina for three months. It starts November 1st. We spoke to the renter in New York and he will be in contact with Eddie who will act on our behalf.

We had a very late lunch at 3:30 pm at the taverna next to a gorgeous theater and restaurant whose name I can't spell or pronounce. I love the building! It is very old-world Czech, lots of gold and art deco and design. We also briefly went to a Cubist Museum nearby which was just okay, kind of disappointing actually. But the building was fabulous. It is art deco designed early 1900 or so and has a spiral stare case of six floors, and originally housed a cafe called "The House of the Black Madonna" where I took pictures. Then, a too long tram, through and out of the city and finally a walk on Weneslas Square, sort of Champs d'Elysees. Peter and I stopped at a MacDonald's where he had a strawberry milk-shake and French fries! MacDonald's is all over Europe. Thankfully.

Just finished packing and will take a very hot bath and drink a glass of wine. Spoke with Eddie and also got several emails all about the horrific events in the US. Very, very depressing and more than a little bit scary. I think I'm having a delayed reaction and feel quite nervous. Peter assures me security will be very tight at the airport and we will be quite safe. I can only pray for this. Tomorrow in the morning at 9 o'clock promptly we'll leave to go see the synagogues and cemetery in the Jewish part of town.

October 4, 2001 — Thursday, 10 AM

We didn't go to Jewish Town. I had an extremely bad night, waking in the middle very nervous with a headache and stomach churning. I couldn't get back to sleep.

I am scared about our country and what our lives are going to be like. It hit me yesterday in a bad way, even though the attack in New York City was three weeks ago. Also, the uncertainty of our future, my health issues and what I have to deal with upon our return are causes for extreme discomfort. I meditated a lot and it seems I feel better if I sit up. I didn't take any pills because I need to be awake and alert for our trip to the synagogue. Peter was comforting but he left for breakfast with the promise to bring me hot water with lemon and didn't return until 10. I wanted to take the 10:58 train to Vienna and now we have to wait until 12:58, which means almost three more hours in this room. It is too rainy to take a walk. I even suggested to Peter that we might return home sooner than planned. I think I need to have this option for my sanity. All of this is discouraging and disturbing to me. But, I am letting go of the "shoulds" — since I'm in Europe I "should" be having a great time all the time, etc. I am also weary. Weary of hotels and restaurants and logistics and asking directions of people who don't speak English and weary of the shitty conditions of our clothes and weary of how I look and feel. Sounds great, right?! I need prayers. Anyway, we don't have the apartment until November 1st so where would we go?

VIENNA REDUX

9:30 PM

A VERY LONG DAY. Ended up taking a 3 pm train to Vienna and had to wait almost three hours in the lamest excuse for a railroad station, and international yet. A porter picked up my duffle bag and ripped it beyond repair. We needed to buy not one but 2 bags at a very small and unattractive store in a station and repack. Got into Vienna at 8 pm, in the room by 8:30 just finished unpacking. This seems like wasted energy for just two days but had to consolidate. Our room at the Savoy is not nearly as nice as the one we had before but still has a lot more charm than the morose Best Western in Prague. We had a lot of frustration with the Pragians, especially at the station where not only do they not speak English but they give so much misinformation that makes the journey unpleasant, to say the least.

October 5, 2001 — Friday, 9 PM

You're not going to believe this. Went down to breakfast this morning. And our friendly guest clerk from our visit a few weeks ago was there and greeted me warmly. I told him how much we liked Vienna and the only thing is we didn't like our room much. He immediately gave me the key to another room # 53,and said "I wonder why you got the room you did." I told him I had already unpacked and we were only staying the one night so it wasn't important to change rooms, but he insisted. "Your last night in Vienna should be spent in a lovely room!" He got a maid to help me move and by the time Peter got back from the market we were completely moved in! Peter was a little shook up as he looked for me in the old room and I wasn't there. He was actually a little panicky. This room is beautiful and most charming in an old-world Viennese way. We left around noon and went to the Museum of Fine Arts and while the art was good, the building was spectacular. I told Peter it was possibly the most beautiful museum I've ever visited. The cafe alone was sumptuous and very grand. The entrance was gorgeous. Lots of marble and a duomo and so much more. I searched in the gift shop for pictures but couldn't find any. I could have sat in the lobby and marveled all day and had a wonderful time.

After a two hour visit and a quick bite, we took a metro to Belvedere which we thought will be yet again another Palace with garden. It turned out to be a Palace turned into an art museum. Peter didn't want to go in so he wandered in the large gardens. After seeing the exhibit of 19 and 20th century arts, I bought him a ticket and made him go in! "You've got to see this!" I proclaimed. There was a room full of art by Egon Schiele the artist whose work we fell in love with at another museum here. Then, two full rooms of Klimpt, including the magnificent "The Kiss." An extraordinary exhibit.

After a bit of a walk through the streets we took a metro to Stephanplatz where we had a fish dinner at a place Peter really liked, right on the square. I like Stephenplatz a lot. It is so alive with stunning shops, street entertainment, well-dressed people. We took another metro to our area where there is an English-speaking movie house. There were three movies playing and Peter wouldn't go to any of them. I would have seen almost anything! We decided to enjoy the room since I have to pack us up and be out by noon tomorrow; I feel like a robot when it comes to packing and unpacking. Or rather I could use one.

October 6, 2001 — Saturday, 9:30 PM Vienna station Wien Sued

Peter is doing his teeth in the bathroom; we are waiting for the train to Venice that leaves at 10:22 pm. Peter and I are bickering. Too much togetherness . We sorely need some time apart.

We left the hotel at noon today. It was a very good idea to have the lovely room at the Savoy and we enjoyed the evening and morning there. After much searching, found a three and a half hour blue Danube, that is actually dirty green, cruise. It left at 2 pm. Made friends with a very nice couple, around our age give or take, and sat with them at a table atop the boat the whole time. Weather not great, chilly and no sun. The cruise itself was a disappointment. We expected to see castles and woods and all we saw was boring scenery. Of some interests were some newish buildings and going through two locks. There were so many other things we could have done here. It was too late to go to Zara or Rosenthal. A day shopping, riding trams and going to flea markets would have been a lot nicer, but how is one to know?

The internet place, hotel for baggage, a cheese sandwich in a waiting room and soon we'll be on the train. I pray it's a warm and safe journey. There is a guy mooching cigarettes from others in this waiting area. We hear that Venice is very crowded and very expensive. Now I'm freezing and in a bad mood.

October 7, 2001 — Sunday, 4 PM

We're in Venice after our usual adventures and misadventures to get here. CNN is on and Peter is in the hall!!! He is wearing nothing but a towel, flossing his teeth!

The train ride was comfortable. I sleep very well when the train is moving and rocking to and fro. The compartment was very modern with all the little amenities including fruits, cookies and water on a table; all this at 10:30 pm. We met four kids, two girls and two boys, backpacking and hosteling it, in a train station at Vienna and they were on the train to Venice and then we saw them again in the early morning and then later on a "Boat Bus!"

October 8, 2001 — Monday, 9 AM

I am writing this in a small sitting room to be found on each of the four floors of this hotel. Peter is doing you know what. This room has old world charm, tea tables, small sofa, and a nice real green plant. I am just noticing that there are nine good size paintings on the wall, but then, typically, one of the walls is decaying and the paint is peeling. The breakfast room was pleasant and the lady who attends to such things changes the white tablecloths after each table is cleared. This is truly a continental breakfast —juice, rolls, coffee, tea or hot chocolate. Fine with me. We didn't leave the room at all since collapsing on the bed at 3 pm. Read a lot, CNN, hot bath, meditation and sleep. The church bells are ringing again. Where am I? Another new place. I read some guide books and it just so much — too much — to see here. I am overwhelmed. There are of course, the "must sees" but I am wont to wander the street and alleyways and avoid the other tourists where possible. Bon chance! There are lots of sounds from the streets. We shut both the windows and the shutters last night and I didn't like the boxed in feeling. I long for my bed, house, and Lucy, all of which I don't have anymore. Time to venture forth.

11:30 PM —

Watching "Bonfire of the Vanities" in Italian of course. Had a really great day. Visited St Mark's Church, the gorgeously gold, Doges Palace, big and tedious, a canal ride on the Grand Canal – beautiful and fun with sightseeing from the water, rest, Vivaldi String Quartet concert at Vivaldi's Church, all young women make up the quartet.

Whipped cream on an already rich cake was music at St Mark's Square. There were two groups alternating at different but nearby cafes, light classics, a great violinist. Sat down for a brandy. And on to bed.

When we arrived at 8:40 am after having breakfast in our compartment (we could choose six items i.e. juice, coffee, yogurts, etc.) We found we had to take a "boat taxi" to our hotel as the train station was on the water not land side. We got ripped off big time. The ride was $45 and we found out later the driver is supposed to bring the suitcase right to the hotel but the driver dumped it and us on the sidewalk. Peter went to find the hotel, leaving me with the bags. An English couple sat me down at a nearby cafe and bought me a cappuccino. So very nice of them. Peter came with a cart that looked like a forklift. The hotel was not far but we had to go over a bridge and steps and down the other side with the cart. Poor Peter is pooped! It's 10 am now and we can't get into the room until noon so we took a walk to St. Mark's Square, which is nearby. The beauty, vastness, and majesty of the Square with trillions of tourists cannot be described. It is a familiar site, lots of movies and television series are filmed here, yet, to be IN it is awesome. We will tour the Cathedral and Doges Palace at a later time. A man approached us and offered us a "free" taxi (boat ride), private to Murano which was said to be 10 minutes away — turned out to be 25 — I timed it. We went because we thought it would be relaxing to just plop on a boat. Silly us!

We landed at a dock adjacent to a glass factory and were greeted and quickly ushered in to watch a master glass blower take nothing, heat it up, and make a beautiful vase. We were ushered into the huge show room of incredibly gorgeous glass objects. I fell in love with all of it. We purchased two small items that ended up being 100 dollars. We had lunch at a nearby restaurant, which was very pleasant. The weather was iffy, cloudy but not cold. Took a boat bus back for free that took one hour. It made many stops and we had to change boats, just like a metro.

I think Venice is astounding; all these great and not so great buildings in the water with little bridges over canals everywhere.

The room is a $150 a night, I think our most expensive hotel yet, and the worst room. Makes the Best Western in Prague seem like the Ritz. There are three beds in here, no carpet, no fridge, a makeshift wood closet, no frills. This is strictly a place to sleep.

And very small. Really a lot of nerve to charge this amount, especially when I think of what we have in Rome for $140 dollars a night. We will rest now and go out later. Maybe.

October 9 mid-day

Left our hotel around noon and headed for the Jewish ghetto. We couldn't go into the synagogue or museum because it's a Jewish holiday. We met a very lovely young Jewish Austrian couple there and we had lunch with them at a kosher restaurant nearby. Turns out, we ate outdoor in a Succoth with a lot of other Jews. I didn't eat much due to the way I am feeling and the fact that I ate a few rolls right before. We took a walk through the streets of Venice with this couple and ended up at an outdoor cafe having beer and talking with them until almost 6 pm.

Peter and I wandered around a bit and then came back to our hotel, which was quite nearby. Looking at a map we will not have made even a dent. Venice is larger than I remembered from my last trip many years ago.

In bed early and reading a Sydney Sheldon book. Tomorrow is our last day here.

Venice is intriguing — the city really does exist on water with lots of boats, there is almost a traffic jam at rush hour! Gondolas, small boat, large boat busses, and private boats. Amazing. Water and bridges everywhere. Have no desire to see more churches, etc. But we'd like to see more of the streets, especially the small canal ways.

October 10, 2001 — Wednesday, 5 PM

Peter and I have decided we are way beyond tired. We operate at about 50% of our usual energy level and we no longer fight this, which is such a relief. Today we got out about 10:15 am and returned to the room at 4:30 pm. We boated, walked and ate. Then we walked and boated again, in two new and different areas. It was delightful. The weather is quite warm, maybe 80 degrees and sunny. No museums, churches or monuments today. We walked into some public park areas and of course, through St. Mark's Square. I ate too much at lunch and I am feeling stuffed three hours later. We are planning on going to the Square later, after resting and packing, for a glass of wine and to hear music. I do want to hear the jazz that is played outdoors in front of one of the restaurants in the Square. We'll see how we feel.

Peter is napping and I am watching "Magnifico Obsessione" in Italian. It is easy to watch a movie in a foreign language when it is one you've already seen. Tomorrow we go to Milan. I sincerely hope the room at the hotel in Milan is nice, something I did not think about much previously, because we are spending more and more time resting.

October 11, 2001 — Thursday, 10:15 AM

Waiting in the room, packed and ready to go. The porter is supposed to show up at 10:15, but then again this is Italy. This is the nightmare part about journey, the schlepping of the luggage made much more difficult since we will be taking a water taxi to the train station. Took a short walk this morning and discovered more alleyways of Venice. There is no end to these mazes. Lots of upscale mostly Italian stores, Ferragamo, Bulgari, Fendi, Laura Biaghotti, Rossetti, Valentino and on and on.

Last night we had a drink at one of the music cafes in the Square, it was a great experience.

We are sitting in St. Mark's Square, with the magnifico Basilica all lit up and the six-piece band playing show tunes and light classics inf front of me, sipping an Orvieto in a temperate climate. Who could want anything more? Not I for sure.

October 12, 2001 – Friday, 9 PM

So much stimulus today! We are on our way to Milan. Left lovely, misty, romantic Venice easily enough via porter, expensive water taxi and then train. We are in a six seat compartment with a 50ish couple from San Francisco. The woman was obnoxious and talked incessantly for the three hour trip. We got an honest cab driver and when we got to our Hotel Guido Peter gave him a large tip for being honest. The hotel is very nice, old fashioned but well kept, large with a very comfortable sitting room, adjacent to the breakfast room. We are up one flight and the room is cozy and charming, of average size. Miracle of miracles, the bathroom has a window with plants on the outer sill. The amazing thing about this room is that there is the exact same Monet print on the opposite side of the bed that we had on our wall in Paris, except that it is smaller, framed and under glass. There are several prints in the room; Monet, Pisarro, Renoir. There is a separate hallway to the bathroom and closet.

I think I am raving about this room because the room we had in Venice was 50% more expensive and completely dismal. We ventured out about 4 pm, had a bite at a nearby bar and then took a tram to the Duomo. Yes, yet another cathedral but what a fabulous church! I'll take pictures tomorrow. We walked to the Galleria Vittorio Emanuel which is an enclosed promenade, has a very very high glass ceiling, dome shaped with a marvelous mosaic floor, full of very expensive shops and restaurants. I very much like the "glass box" restaurants. You can be private and yet see out. We had a small dinner and then went to yet another internet place. We attempted a tram back.

A very adorable and funny incident.

We asked the girl sitting next to us for directions showing her the address of the hotel and before we knew it, the whole bus got involved in finding out how we should travel. It was quite touching. We planned on going on a city tour tomorrow, but we are tired and the tour is very early, so we may just hang out and I will take a tour of La Scala and window shop at Armani. Armani is king here. Bath time.

October 12, 2001 – Friday 8:30 pm

No mention of Columbus Day by the Italians. Go figure. I am splurging on notepaper and have this whole book and just two weeks left on this seemingly never-ending saga. Before I get into the splendors of the day, I just laid out the clothes I wore. I like to air out my clothes before putting them away since they don't get cleaned often obviously. I see that the beige sweater came from Venice, the black pants from Stratford, the red shoes from Capri, the belt purchased today in Milan matches the shoes, from a kiosk and the young man showed me "this is how they wear it in Italy" which is way down on the hips! My purse is old but it came from Portugal. I feel so international.

Peter and I took a tram ride and I told him to keep an eye out for a hairdresser and lo and behold! A Jean Louis David shop appeared. We hopped off the train at 5 pm and entered. One lady spoke a little English, I explained to her what I wanted, roots and highlights. She said she could do it right away and it will take about two hours. Peter said "Do it!" and took off. A very strange procedure, but I just said, oh well. Now I find I have not only color but a completely different hair style. It is longer now so she blow dried it with a round brush; haven't had this done in years. Purchased some products and $125 later felt the shop feeling a bit more attractive. Peter says I look very European. I like that, what I think it means.

Peter and I split up for a few hours. Necessary. I walked Victor Emanuel II and then Via Spigia and saw all the great shops and haute couture houses. I found Armani, not the store but his actual working office and factory. A man dressed in black (of course) was at the gate inside a beautiful courtyard that led to the entrance of the venue. He was polite but firm. He served the purpose of keeping Cinderella types like me out. He told me where the new Armani store was nearby. I went in and it was fantastic. A large space, maybe a square block with three floors, including electronics, a café, florist and clothes. I just had to have something from Armani in Milan; I purchased a plain black tee shirt from the men's department for about $44. So today was expensive. Had lunch at a little café on VEII and noted that the salad was $7. This was a good deal and I had a medium size beer with it. The beer was $6.50, almost as much as the salad. My heart skipped a beat when I saw that "Moulin Rouge" was playing nearby, but alas and alack, in Italian.

Met Peter and we took a tour of the magnifico La Scala and its museums. There was a Steinway piano on exhibit which was a gift from the opera house to Liszt. It said "do not touch" so of course I had to skim my fingers very lightly over the keys. My fingers touched the same piano keys as did Liszt! I swear my fingers were tingling. Peter did not believe I did this! I like Milan a lot, it's a real city. And this is what I like best. I told Peter "Europe is about four things: art, music, food and shopping."

The Milanese women are trampy chic. They wear beautiful, high fashion clothes, very tight fitting, short skirts, high heels, fishnet or black stockings, tons of hair and jewelry. Peter says "Fishnet wouldn't be appropriate in Culver City." Ha ha.

October 13, 2001

Just had breakfast. I like this room and wanted to eat here at least once. I reiterate that I like this hotel a lot, it really has old world charm without old world opulence. Our room is bright apricot, and it's nice to be away from white walls. Two weeks from tomorrow we leave for home. Some of the actual terror of this has left me and now this is sadness settle in that soon the European flavor and experience will be gone. I love Europe and could spend the rest of my life living here while making trips every two months back to the States to see everyone. This sounds ideal, right? Despite the inconveniences, the magical feeling stays with me.

Observation. My parents were Europeans and I am a Mediterannean café dweller at heart. I mostly like everything we've done here, but I know I need more structure and responsibility; without plans I feel mostly uncomfortable. I sorely miss things like weekly market trips, yoga classes, piano, docent work at LACMA, etc. And friends and family, of course.

Life on the westside of Los Angeles would be a huge adjustment. After 20 years in the Valley and my support there, now it is new people and places to adjust to. I am sure I will be making many trips to the Valley, at least for several months. I will need to wean myself from doctors, hairdressers, manicurists, and Nordstrom's. I think it can be the best of both worlds, the comfortable and the familiar with something different but not completely unknown. We have met many people in the past six months. I am sorry I didn't get more email addresses. Correspondence is my thing and certainly made easy with the internet.

Today we will hang out around Milan doing this and that. We no longer care to visit churches, museums or monuments. I said that before but when we come across these venues, I cannot help but enter. A beautiful and restful park would be nice and a long train ride where we would have comfy seats. We leave for Florence tomorrow and there is so much art there. Returning to Rome will be a rest! Isn't that weird. I shall enjoy just hanging out, doing some spa stuff, gift shopping and knowing me, I will get away from Peter and visit a museum or two knowing it's the last hurrah.

7:30 pm

Back in our room. We left around 11 am and took a tram to the Duomo. We noticed a large and orderly crowd in back of the church. We asked several people about this but no one spoke English. It seems that the President of the Republic was inside attending a memorial service for the Italians who died in New York City and DC during the 9/11 siege. It was said that there were about 200 Italians missing. The President came out and as his car drove by, I got a quick picture of his wife waving from the car, quite close up.

As the observatory at the Duomo is closed due to this event, we took the number 14 tram for a ride. Turns out we ended up in an ugly and poor neighborhood. We got up and out and took a very new and modern tram in the other direction to a nicer area, where we visited a flea market. Peter bought apricots, prunes and walnuts. We looked for a place to have lunch and ended up at an outdoor restaurant near the Duomo and actually finished having lunch at 4 pm. We went up to the top of the Duomo and walked on the rooftop of the church. This is truly an amazing sight which included tops of actual spires and statues atop the church. It was a gorgeous sunny day, tee shirt weather. We walked all around the roof, in and out of corridors and took lots of pictures. After a short sit in front of the church, watching a lot of activity, we took a walk near La Scala and found ourself on a lovely street called Via Brera, full of large shops and restaurants and museums. We caught the number 4 tram to our street and Peter found a very happening street nearby full of Chinese shops and restaurants. Wish I knew about this area earlier before spending precious time doing something I ended up not liking. Peter says there are no mistakes, just experiences. He has such a good philosophy about life. Milan is a good city, there is lots to see and do. Different and modern and old all at the same time. Tomorrow we leave noon for Florence. I am reading my second John Grisham book and it's gripping. Since there ' is no TV, these books are a God send. Early to sleep, I hope. Park in early am.

October 14, 2001 — Sunday, 12:30 PM

We are on the train to Florence. Peter is across from me sleeping. Next to each of us, in the aisle seats are two ladies, surely in their 80's. They aren't talking. Their children, married to each other, put them on this train with a few pieces of small luggage. The women were crying softly as they waved goodbye to their children on the platform. They probably don't live far away and near enough for visit by train. I later found out the women are from Naples, which is really not close at all.

We had an eventful start today. We packed early and then took a walk and came upon a cemetery, very near to our hotel; Cimentario Monumentale, or something like that. We went in and we're completely bowled over by what we saw, burial crypts that were the size of small houses and beautiful landscapes with statuary and when looking at a map, the name of the designers and architects of each crypt was listed! We found a Jewish section much to our surprise with menorahs and stars, very tastefully done. Large open spaces, too, between each burial place. Many distinguished families have burial plots the size of a car garage.

FLORENCE

The train is completely full and we will make many stops. I have no idea where Florence is in the lineup. The ladies are now eating sandwiches they brought on board and have offered me bites, which I graciously refused. Peter continues to rest but will wake up at each stop, he says, to check the luggage which sits on the floors between cars. After lugging all the stuff through Europe, it will be horrible to have it stolen.

8:30 PM

We are in a hotel room from hell. But thankfully we will only be here this one night. We arrived well enough in Florence in three hours' time and got to our hotel quickly.

From the outside the hotel looked okay. But! As soon as I saw the room, I told Peter "I can't stay here!" He agreed. The room is extremely small, no amenities, no pictures, no drawers, and might work for one person if they put only a single bed in.

Although tired, we left by cab to the Centrico to check out other hotels but had no clue as to where to even begin as the tourist office closes early on Sunday. After lots of walking and wheel spinning, we found a three-star hotel on the Arno River. We didn't see the room, just a picture, but we saw the lobby, which is quite nice, and the location is good. Supposedly we can walk everywhere of interest. Supposedly. We trudged around looking for a place to eat, which at 6 pm is difficult. Nothing opens until later. We found an adorable trattoria. I had ribalto, a Florentine dish made of vegetables and bread that looked like soup. We took a taxi back to our hotel. Tomorrow, too, we will have to take a taxi to our new hotel and then we're going to do laundry at last which means two more taxis. We have a ton of dirty clothes. I am actually looking forward to this!

My first impression of Florence is that it is extremely crowded and not too clean. Hopefully, once we explore the beauty of the city, my opinion will change. I also think it's probably very expensive here. I shall behave but I do intend to shop. Tomorrow after our chores we will find out about tours within the city and to Sienna and tickets to the Ufizzi. This awful hotel at least has a bathtub.

October 15, 2001 — Monday, 10 PM

Believe it or not, we just got in from having dinner. Yes! We actually had dinner in a restaurant at the hour the Italians eat.

To back track a bit, the hotel room from hell was freezing last night and we got little sleep. Arose, dressed and out by 9 am. Brought our stuff over to our new hotel which is called Hotel Privilege, dropped everything off and did laundry. Returned to the hotel by noon and found we couldn't get in to our room until 2 pm. We took a walk on the Ponte Vecchio; the ultimate in tourist traps for jewelry and walked to the Pitti palace. I expected a lot of tourism on the Ponte Vecchio but also remembered from thirty years ago how old and beautiful the little shops were. I guess they are still there, but there is so much merchandise and so many people it's hard to see the buildings.

The day turned hot, just like yesterday, in the afternoon. We got into our room at 2 pm and boy! Do I ever love it! What a huge difference from where we spent last night and just $20 more a night. There are only 18 rooms in what was an 18th century villa. Our room faces the Arno (and never-ending traffic.) Our windows are triple paned and I still hear the motorcycles. The room is very large; I think a bit bigger than our whole apartment in Rome. We were greeted by fabric mats next to each of our side of the bed on the floor and slippers. We have a seating area with two large gray fabric chairs and a table. And we have a daybed/

couch in addition to our bed. Also, a radio. This is most unusual. We have always had TV but not ever radio. There is a big closet, refrigerator, TV and the usual stuff. We rested (read: Peter slept and I unpacked) and I rested and bathed and then we went out about 7 pm. We went to a restaurant nearby recommended in Fodor's. We were too early, as they don't open until 8 pm and without trying as we did for an hour last night, found a restaurant in the nearby Hotel Cavour, which looked very nice and had a doorman and a large lobby. At dinner, a young couple sat down next to us outdoors and after dinner they talked with us. This was slightly embarrassing to me because all throughout dinner they were talking German and I had no idea they spoke English. I commented to Peter that they were going to eat a lot more than we would but that they were young and could handle it. Don't know if they heard or not.

They were very nice and were from Switzerland. So, there's the day. Tomorrow our plan is to visit the synagogue and its museum, shop for shoes for Peter and gifts and generally see the city. Peter wants to sleep late tomorrow. We'll see how that goes.

October 16, 2001 — Tuesday, 7:30 PM

Just got back from our day out. Awoke at 7:30 am and not knowing the time I thought it was about 3 in the morning, so I took a sleeping pill. About ten seconds after I took the pill the alarm went off and Peter told me it was 7:30 am. Oops. What to do? I laid in in bed until almost 9 and then feeling very doped up, got up and attempted to ignore this stoned feeling. We had a lovely breakfast, and while eating, I told Peter this is the best breakfast we have had on this voyage, and the room is charming as well. Didn't leave the hotel until after 11 am.

Took a bus after walking across a bridge over the Arno which in fact, was very thrilling! to Piazzle Michaelangelo. There were about a dozen tour buses on at the top of the Piazzle. It afforded us a magnifico view of the city. We spotted our hotel almost directly across, on the other side of the river, but much lower down. We walked on Via Belvedere down. Stopped at a beautiful church on a hill, to Forte Belvedere and further downhill to the Palazzo Pitti in our intent to see the Boboli Gardens. We had lunch at a café in the Palace and then walked about a million steps up the top of the Gardens and had many beautiful views.

After our visit, we walked over the Ponte Vecchio and then we took a bus which took us to a very non tourist area of discount shops recommended by Barbara, our wonderful concierge. Peter actually bought a pair of shoes. Peter buying clothing for himself is huge. I wanted him to buy more but he didn't find anything he wanted. We took a bus back to the Duomo, which was closed and went to Via Calziole which is a main drag and bought wallets for Eddie and Henry. We ate "I'm having ice cream for dinner," I tell Peter, at a nearby cafeteria and walked back to the hotel. Notice the trend here? Walk, walk, walk. Tomorrow we go to Sienna.

October 17, 2001 – Wednesday 7:00 pm

Only 7:00 pm and we are ready to pass out. Just got in from a day that started at 7:00 am when we got up, out and at the hotel next door by 8:30 for our bus trip to Sienna and San Gimignano. Arrived at San Gimignano around 10:30 and were let loose from our bus for an hour. This is a most interesting, different city and I would have liked to spend more time here. The old part of the city is completely walled in by stone and all the buildings are stone including several museums and churches. Big surprise. We got to Sienna around 12:30 and eight of us and a tour guide ate at a restaurant recommended by her but she didn't sit with us. Lunch was not very tasty. We met our tour guide at 2 pm at the Piazzle Campo, the main and maybe biggest square we've seen yet in all of our travels. The tour took us almost immediately to the Duomo and then to a religious museum near the church. Then back to the bus, arriving in Firenze near 6 pm. What I enjoyed most was the ride as we passed through little villages and Chianti wine country. We went for tea and little sandwiches at Rivoire, a chic outdoor and indoor café at Signorina Square, an interesting area, empty except for, around the periphery, many large and beautiful statues. The Ufizzi Palazzo gallery borders the square. Walked through yet another upscale shopping street and will now take a hot bath, have Peter massage my aching back and go to bed with John Grisham. Tomorrow, synagogue and Ufizzi Gallery.

October 18, 2001 – Thursday 7:30 pm

Today we left around 10 am for the synagogue which turned out to be only 15 minutes away. The weather is outstanding; warm and sunny and very unlike what usually occurs mid-October; rain.

The synagogue is stunning. It is mosaic and Moroccan in feeling, large and home to about 1,000 Florentine Jews. Unfortunately, we were not allowed to take pictures but we purchased an illustrated brochure. We then went to the Academia dell Art where I waited 20 minutes on line to see Michaelangelo's David. There were not many people in this gallery and I got myself a seat. I just stared at this magnificent sculpture for an hour. He is much more than splendid.

There is a modern functional chair and I'm sitting on it. Glorious David is directly in front of me, about 20 feet away, very large on a six-foot pedestal with a natural light from the cupola shining down on him. He is much more than wonderful; he is luminous. The world knows he is not in perfect proportion, his right hand in particular is overly large and one can barely see the slingshot. He looks quite intelligent and one gets the sense that this intelligence rather than brute force is what brought Goliath down. Most of the onlookers appeared to be here just to see him as I am. I would give a cursory look to the other art as long as I am here, but David is so magnifico, it is enough to sit in his wake and marvel at Michaelangelo's brilliance.

Peter and I met up in San Marco Park where we had a pasta lunch in the garden room of a nearby café. We walked to the Duomo, went in, sat on a bench at the periphery and closed our eyes for 45 minutes. I was not impressed by the Duomo, those in Milan and Sienna are far more spectacular. Peter walked me to the Ufizzi Gallery where I spent about 90 minutes while he did his email at the internet café. Tomorrow at 10:00 am I am going to the local Jean Louis David salon and once again attempt to have highlights put in my ever- darkening hair for 92000 liras. The news on CNN stinks and now there is an anthrax scare. I shall double dose my Xanax on my flight home. Now, the bath.

October 19, 2001 – Friday 7:30 pm

Another busy day. Had a good night's sleep after watching an American movie I never heard of in Italian and reading Elle Magazine at the same time. We had room service which we didn't expect, at 8:00 a.m. I ordered poached eggs. I had just finished doing yoga. I don't do enough yoga. My back gave me some pain last night and I had a headache. Today I felt good and kept my hair appointment. Peter and I had a day apart. It was like an Abbot and Costello routine, three people who don't speak English plus a fourth brought from another shop to interpret, figured out, sort of, what I wanted done to my hair. I let the operator work on me with much trepidation. I left the shop with a wet head so had no clue until my hair dried as to what it would look like. The things at home we take for granted.

At noon I did window shopping in a chichi area and then had lunch at a very nice outdoor café at the Piazza Republica. I am convinced no one in Europe eats indoors.

A young Parisian couple sat next to me and with a large beer in me, I had the courage to speak with them in French. I miss hearing French a lot. After they left, I devoted myself to listening to four American women from Michigan discuss their marriages, get their bill and involve the waiter in a serious discussion about who owes what to whom. Quite funny. I meandered after around Buena Nueva and got lost but loved walking because of great weather and feeling a bit high. Walked over the Arno by the Piazza Goldini Bridge and found, lo and behold! a small designer jewelry store, where everything was plastic and gorgeous. This, in the land of leather. I am going to check this place out further domani. I need nothing. I bought a small and cheap Florentine purse. That's it.

Joined up with Peter at 4:30 in front of the Duomo as planned. We shopped and Peter purchased two belts from a street vendor. Peter had pasta at yet another cafeteria near the Duomo and we went our way back to the hotel. Our lovely concierge Barbara says it will rain tomorrow. We may go to Fiesole because other than shopping and museums what do you do in Florence? I couldn't get Peter to a museum here on a bet as he doesn't like religious art at all. Florence is for art and leather lovers. I decided there is no difference between the street and the sidewalk. Cars and pedestrians on both. Enough said. Buonasera.

October 20, 2001 – Saturday PM

I am feeling sad about leaving Florence. I shall miss Barbara; our large lovely room overlooking the Arno and the sights and smells of Florence but not the sounds of all the traffic.

We went to a large park around noon, after some creative purchases of interesting jewelry from the shop on the other side of the river I previously visited. We got stupid bus directions to the park and I will be glad not to have to deal with logistics beyond next week. We watched some men play soccer. When we left I applauded and they all laughed. We took the number 7 bus to Fisole, an adorable town of 15,000 people, some 6 miles straight up. We visited a Roman amphitheater that dates back to the first century AD, excellently renovated and restored. It was eerie and awesome to sit in these seats of stone. They don't tear anything down in Europe. I deeply respect their reverence for the old. Returned from dinner at the trattoria where we had our dinner the first night here. Once again had ribalto, and beer and fruit salad. Have to pack tonight but must rest first; I can barely stand up.

ARRIVERDERCI ROMA

October 21, 2001 – Sunday 7:30 pm

We are back at Mayfair Residence in Rome. We have a most unusual apartment that consists of a large living room with an iron spiral staircase at one end, and that leads to an equally large bedroom on the second level. We have a terrace on each floor. The first apartment we had here was prettier as the furnishings were nicer, but it was less than half the size of this one. We also have a TV on each floor, which right now is a good thing. We are both worn out and Peter says it is time for us to go home.

I have no idea what we will be doing in Rome, this, our last week in Europe. I took a short walk to Via Veneto and had a very expensive cup of tea at Doney. We are watching MTV which is showing an all-star tribute to the firefighters and police of September 11. Every famous or semi famous person from New York is on this show. Jerry Seinfeld and Woody Allen made short films about New York City and Howard Stern appeared in person. Nothing else to say. Saying goodbye to Barbara yesterday was sad but we get to see Sara, our friend here at the Mayfair.

October 22, 2001 – Monday 10 pm

I see that my routine has already changed. I was reading my third John Grisham book and suddenly realized not only had I almost forgotten to write in this book for the second night in a row I didn't take a bath. Something I do religiously every night.

Today was ho-hum. Being in Rome now is more comforting than it is exciting. This may be a good thing. Finished unpacking and didn't leave here until noon. Met Peter at internet place at 12:30. It was nice walking down Via Veneto in gorgeous weather. Took the #116 electric bus to Piazza Barborini as if the six weeks since we left here never happened. That is, until we got to the American Embassy which is right on the Via Veneto. It is UNAPPROACHABLE due to the atrocity in New York, barriers all around and lots of armed guards. Tanks even. We took a walk to Trevi to see our friend Tanni handing out flyers on the street.

She was happy to see us. We had a small pasta lunch and then walked to the Spanish Steps. Peter left me and I strolled to Piazza del Popolo, trammed back to the internet café when I sent my final Europe emails.

Purchased an ice cream, walked back to the hotel and got flowers on the way. Returned and found that Peter's business appointment hadn't shown up yet. His plane from London was delayed and he showed up close to 7 pm and left at 8:15. We had a visitor! I made tea and cookies. Tomorrow we are going to do some wandering and then – tada! Going to see the new Woody Allen movie. Prayers for all.

October 23, 2001 – Tuesday 4:15 PM

I am sitting up in bed because if I lay down, I will fall asleep. I had a beer about an hour ago on an empty stomach and although I hastily returned to our apartment and wolfed down a salad and several crackers, I feel zonked.

We left early today, around 9:00 am and headed for the Via Appia Antica, the first road built in Rome and the trip took around 90 minutes. We walked around until noon and I found it interesting. We saw a very old church with no interior, a huge mausoleum and fort. We started to return to the Centro at noon. We waited 40 minutes for a bus and then took the metro to the very old San Giovanni area, a church and lots of stores in the area. Peter is kind of ho hum at this stage and so am I, but I fight it because I know that in just a few days' time we will no longer have the sights and smells of Europe. We took a metro to American Express at Piazza di Spagna to inquire about a tour for tomorrow to Villa d'Este and Hadrian's Villa. Peter doesn't want to go but will since he promised me this trip some time back. I have mixed feelings but I definitely want to do something. Thursday I will have my day alone and I have made a reservation at the Borghese Galleries. We are having dinner with Carole Hazzard at one of the "glass box" restaurants on Via Veneto. We placed two phone calls to Franco, the Erte exhibitor, and left messages on his machines. I fear the evening of jazz will not happen. We are going to the Woody Allen movie tonight, hopefully.

October 24, 2001 – Wednesday 8:15 PM

At 5:30 we met a couple, on the Via Veneto near the food market, got to talking and ended up having a glass of wine with them at Harry's Bar outdoors on Via Veneto. I remember thinking how pleasant and how natural it is to casually sit down and see loveliness everywhere; the walls of the Borghese Gardens, the Via Veneto, all in fabulous weather. I shall sorely miss this. Actually, I shall sorely miss a lot of what we've seen in Europe. Last night we had an awful time trying to get to the movie theater. After a few busses and a lot of back tracking we got there in 90 minutes. We were too late for the 6:30 show so Peter said we would go to the 8:30, he was determined we would see a movie in a theater after all it took to get there. At one point I actually started to cry from frustration and disappointment. We spent over an hour sitting at a very hip non touristy café, drinking tea. The theater was down an alleyway. It looked very small but inside it was ultra-modern with a large screen, but not many seats. We discovered we were in an artistic complex, and next to the theater we heard cello and violin music. There was a small legit theater and a bistro nearby. The theater was freezing but I was just happy to see a movie, albeit not one of Woody Allen's best, at long last.

We took a taxi back and the ride took less than ten minutes! I didn't leave the apartment until noon today. I met Peter and we went to see the Klimpt, Kokosha, Schiele exhibit at a smallish museum at the back of Victor Emmanuel, on a hill overlooking the Forum. Each painting was a winner. Lunch at nearby café; pasta of course.

Then we took a metro to Via Flamina which was a disappointment, but before that we went to see a bones exhibit which was extraordinary. There were over 4000 skulls and bones in five rooms, displayed artfully in an old cemetery building. It seems that in the 1700s three Capucine monks set about to honor the 4000 monks who died and retrieved their remains from various cemeteries. An astonishing feat that took the three monks their entire lifetimes to accomplish.

Tomorrow we have separate days. I have a nine am reservation at the Borghese Galleries and then I will shop and have a nice lunch somewhere. My favorite way to spend the day. We are having dinner with Carole Hazzard tomorrow night. I decided I really like this two-floor apartment as it gives us much needed privacy.

October 25, 2001 – Thursday almost midnight

An almost perfect day. I fall more in love with Rome as the days remaining here fly by. I awoke at 6:45 showered, put on my lounging dress and went to the lobby, determined to see Max, our loveable concierge. "Hi Max!" We greeted each other warmly, chatted a bit. Did some yoga. I am stiff as a board. Had breakfast with Peter and he walked me to the Villa Borghese. We arrived at 8:45 am. I stayed until noon. The exhibit of Bernini sculptures was almost too beautiful to bear. I broke my cardinal rule of no museum brochures because there were so many things I loved, especially the statue of Daphne and Apollo. I purchased a print which is a reproduction of a drawing of the sculpture and will frame and hang it when I get home. Wherever home will be, that is. I sat in the lovely garden in the back after having a capuccino in the museum.

Then, I walked past the Borghese woods through the wall on to the Via Veneto where I took a good old 116 electric bus to Piazza di Spagna. Only! I daydreamed past the stop and ended up in an unknown area. I walked around, following signs and found myself at the very top of the Spanish Steps, very near the hotel where Bill Clinton is staying. Walked down the steps and had lunch at an outdoor café (is there any other kind?) on Via Frattine, a very fashionable shopping street. I wandered around there and Via Condotti, bought zero and got back to the apartment near 3:30 pm. I purchased some daisies for the apartment and a fuschia plant for Sara. She was thrilled by this gesture.

Franco, the Erte exhibitor, phoned and it was decided that we would meet Carole at the Erte exhibit as another American type group was playing music there. Franco met us, brought us in and we stayed for the entire concert. I had mixed feelings about the music. Franco took us out for a drink at a place called Gasto. It was very large on multi levels, indoor and out, very noisy and not conducive to conversation. We left at 11 pm just as a three-piece combo was starting to play. I enjoyed today a lot. I am pleasantly tired. Tomorrow we shop for gifts.

I am the only woman in Rome who doesn't own a red leather jacket.

October 26, 2001 – Friday, 9:45 pm

I am depressed about leaving? Going home? This is not an expected emotion. I've been looking forward to being back home, with friends and family and the comfort of a known territory. But! I sense that so much is OVER – the planning, the expectations, the challenges and delight of a new city – no more. We started packing and it hit me that we are not packing to go to another city in Europe. Rome is comfortable now. And now we leave. No more cafes, ruins, parks, museums et al. And it has to be said, no more noise and crowds and dirt and rude people and language problems and food issues. But it is harder leaving that I would have thought.

I purchased a cross at the gift shop at the Vatican for Marjorie and now I can't find it. What else have I lost? I wonder. So much packing, unpacking and moving around.

We arose late today and left around noon. We did our final and big gift shopping with no problems and I like our purchases. Got back around 5 pm, rested a bit, and started packing. Had dinner at the restaurant across the street and met a young man named Karl from Eugene, Oregon. His father was a football coach at the University of Oregon, Peter's alma mater. Peter was thrilled to talk with him. Tomorrow we are having a picnic at Borghese Gardens with Carole. I shall go to the market while Peter makes his final internet visit. If there is time and energy, we will go to Piazza Navona for a final walk tomorrow night. We have to get to bed early as our plane leaves at 7:45 am! and we need to leave for the airport at 4:30 am.

Tomorrow is our last day in Rome, our last day in Europe. So hard to believe that six months have come and gone. Okay, that's a cliché. I recognize that.

October 27, 2002 – Saturday, 4:00 pm

THE LAST DAY. Found out this morning that Italy goes on standard time tonight as well as the USA, so we put back the clock an hour and to get a well needed extra hours sleep. A car is picking is up at 4:30 am, about 12 hours from now. Awoke today still sad about leaving. It is really hitting me hard. I am so accustomed to being in Europe. I fear that in a few days it will be just a big dream. Did a little shopping in the neighborhood as I had to get rid of extra liras, and bought Peter a sweater. Went in and out of shops and discovered a whole new neighborhood in the opposite direction of where we usually head. Got the picnic together and met Peter and Carole at the Borghese Gardens. Such a heavenly place. We had a pleasant afternoon and I probably drank too much vino. Resting now and going to Piazza Navona for a last look. My favorite piazza in Rome. Peter told me he is going to miss having the bed made every day and the apartment cleaned. I wonder what he means by this. Hmmm..... Rest now.

9:45 PM

We left here at 7 pm and went to Piazza Navona for a last stroll. The sculptures and gushing fountains are feats of magical artistry. So many fountains in Rome. But this is the most beautiful,

I think. We walked yet another new neighborhood; is there ever an end to new neighborhoods? Back to the hotel. Said goodbye to Sara which was sad for all concerned. I muse on the fact that we've made many friends in our travels of the people who work for or around us. Sara hugged us and told us that saying goodbye is the difficult part of the job but something she had to do all the time. As with others we exchanged email addresses.

I was quite nervous a while ago but feel calmer now. It took us almost two days to finish shopping and packing to leave. I hope and pray for a safe return to our home country. We are a bit leery considering the disaster of 9/11. Peter is ready to go home and asked me if I could stay another month would I, and I said no. I want to go home as well. I am worn out! And I need structure in my life, despite the issues that lay ahead. There will be many. There are so many, already, wonderous memories from the first day we arrived in magical Paris and how thrilled we were to be on this adventure.

LOS ANGELES

And now we are back in the United States. It feels weird. We will be in our rental apartment in the Marina while we look for our new home. We will rest. And rest. And think about the past six months. I am in awe of the fact that we did this! And how this trip has changed our outlook on life. Which it has. We are reconnecting with family and friends. We are getting a new phone number! A new address! New checkbooks!

The next adventure has already begun. Ne c'est pas?